CALL TO GREATNESS

The material in this book is taken from the Godkin Lectures delivered at Harvard University, March, 1954 under the title of "A Troubled World."

CALL TO GREATNESS

BY ADLAI E. STEVENSON

NEW YORK

HARPER & BROTHERS PUBLISHERS

Library of Congress catalog card number: 54-6028

To my good companions on a long and mem-
orable journey around the world in 1953:
Walter Johnson, Barry Bingham, William McC.
Blair, Jr., and William Attwood.

Foreword

AT Harvard University in March of 1954 I talked to the students and faculty about the troubled world in which we live. Many people who have some authority, and more who have none, are writing and talking incessantly about foreign affairs these days. While I make no pretense to superior wisdom in this field, there were at least three reasons why I presumed to do likewise at Harvard: in the first place, because I have been much interested in our neighbors since a childhood residence in Europe; secondly, because in 1953 I traveled through thirty countries along the free side of the iron curtain from Seoul to Berlin; and, finally, because our foreign affairs are, of course, our most important public affairs.

My purpose was to sketch the genesis and set in some crude historical perspective the present troubled world scene, and then to attempt to defrost a tiny segment of the opaque window through which we see others and others see us—and to do it briefly, having listened to many lectures myself!

I was not content with the result at the time, and I am less so now after re-reading them two months later. My excuse is the pressure of competing work, including a book about my travels last year which was finished this spring and promptly abandoned. It was a hard decision, but I am sure I will not regret that it was never published. I wish I could be equally sure that I will not regret that these lectures were published! Perhaps the circumstances of their writing, however, are better described in the following introductory remarks to the audience at Harvard University on the evening of March 17, 1954:

"More than a year ago in a light-hearted, careless moment I accepted your invitation to give the Godkin lectures this year. I have been regretting it acutely of late—while trying to prepare something for you and at the same time keep abreast of my other work, my mail, my visitors, the telephone, the newspapers—and the Republicans! Moreover, I fear that I have spent more time wondering nervously why I undertook to do these lectures than in doing them. My conclusion, in case you are interested in the rise and fall of political meteors, is that after the election of 1952, with gracious and intoxicating applause ringing in my ears from many centers of learning, my lecturing at Harvard did not seem as absurd to me as it does now, and as it shortly will to you, I fear.

"Confronted, surrounded indeed, as I am here in Cambridge tonight by more highly educated fellow citizens than I have ever faced, and inadequately prepared, I am uncomfortably reminded of the abiding truth of those classic words that never occurred to Horace: 'Via ovicipitum dura est,' or, for the benefit of the engineers among you: 'The way of the egghead is hard.'

"At first, I thought I would talk to you about state government in our scheme of things—a subject which I had a rare opportunity to learn something about as one who was elected Governor of a great state without any prior political experience. It was also a subject entirely consistent with the terms of the gift creating this, the Godkin lectureship: 'On the Essentials of Free Government and the Duties of the Citizen.' But instead of talking about state government, which I do know something about, I am going to talk about the troubled age we live in, which many of you know a great deal more about.

"So I have compounded the indiscretion of speaking here at all with an imprudent choice of subject. But in spite of the fact that world affairs fill your press, your journals and forums, I concluded to talk about the same thing because it seems to me that the historic drama of the twentieth century in which we are inextricably involved dwarfs in immensity all our other concerns, and places in new perspective 'the essentials of free government and the duties of the citizen.' "

Thereupon, and for three successive evenings, I belabored the gracious audience as hereafter set forth.

Libertyville, Illinois   ADLAI E. STEVENSON
May 30, 1954

CALL TO GREATNESS

Ordeal
of the Mid-Century

GREAT movements and forces, springing from deep wells, have converged at this mid-century point, and I suspect we have barely begun to comprehend what has happened and why. In the foreground is the mortal contest with world communism, which is apparent, if the means of dealing with it are not always apparent. But in the background are the opaque, moving forms and shadows of a world revolution, of which communism is more the scavenger than the inspiration; a world in transition from an age with which we are familiar to an age shrouded in mist. We Americans have to deal with both the foreground and the background of this troubled, anxious age.

It is easy to state our ends, our goals, but it is hard

1

to fit them to our means. Every day, for example, politicians, of which there are plenty, swear eternal devotion to the ends of peace and security. They always remind me of the elder Holmes' apostrophe to a katydid: "Thou say'st an undisputed thing in such a solemn way." And every day statesmen, of which there are few, must struggle with limited means to achieve these unlimited ends, both in fact and in understanding. For the nation's purposes always exceed its means, and it is finding a balance between means and ends that is the heart of foreign policy and that makes it such a speculative, uncertain business.

We thought and hoped we had found it. After all the struggle and sacrifice of two world wars to fence in the mad dogs and preserve peace and security, we thought the reward was calm and the enjoyment of the fruits of our exertions. History seems to record such intervals of confidence, security, dignity as the fitting conclusion of great exertion—the Augustan Age of Rome, the France of the Grand Monarch, and Victoria's England. But whether serenity was the interest on past or current investments, such gentle grace has not been our lot in the twentieth century. Instead the first and second planetary wars have helped to make of this half century the most barbaric interval of the Christian era, branded with the restoration of slavery and torture, the destruction of whole cities and the extermination of tens of millions of our fellow men, far more indeed than in the past thousand years.

History has not stood still for us. Instead it has moved faster than ever before, and with the development of the H-bomb and the ferment of revolution spreading from Asia to Africa, history's dizzy pace shows no signs of moderating.

So now, at mid-century, we talk about the land hunger of the Indian peasant and read of Communists in Guatemala and terrorists in Kenya as though they were all citizens of Illinois. It is the same abroad. For those who can read and the many more who can listen, our words and deeds in Washington are as significant in Delhi, Moscow and Jakarta as they are in Boston, but they are not as well understood.

There was a time, and it was only yesterday, when the United States could and did stand aloof. In the days of our national youth Washington warned against "entangling alliances," John Adams spoke of that "system of neutrality and impartiality" which was to serve us long and well, and Jefferson enumerated among our blessings that we were "kindly separated by nature and a wide ocean from the exterminating havoc of one quarter of the globe." But those days are gone forever. They ended when the First World War began just forty years ago. The youngest Republic is now the oldest, and if life begins at forty, the circumstances of middle age are nonetheless hard and in many ways disappointing.

Once we were weak and stood apart; now we are powerful and permanently involved. Once we were un-committed and the New World was called upon to redress the balance of the Old; now we are committed and the job of maintaining the balance is at once less glamorous and more importunate than an occasional call to tip the scales. The world at our mid-century is, as someone has said, like a drum—strike it anywhere and it resounds everywhere. The problems of peoples whom we scarcely knew existed, unless we read the *National Geographic*, now resound in our ears and sap our strength, and also our patience. And those distant peoples have suddenly become aware that they too are not masters of their own destiny; that their future, their history, is inseparable from ours. The boundless main is no longer the safeguard of our remove but the measure of our employ.

The world has endured violent and unprecedented dislocations in this past half century of technological, political and social revolution. For us the shock has been severe and in great depth. Conditioned as we have been for a hundred years to the growth, enrich-ment and development of a continent in security behind our ocean barriers, for most Americans a successful foreign policy would be one which did not involve us in foreign affairs. The ideal is total isolation. But the reality is total and permanent involvement with all mankind.

For many of us our new dimensions are still incomprehensible. For many the idea that we are no longer wholly dependent on ourselves but also on masses of Europeans, Africans, Asians and Latin Americans is not only distasteful but incredible. And for everyone confrontation everywhere by the implacable hostility of the Communist conspiracy is exasperating and frightening. The bright expectations of the moment of victory, of V-E Day and V-J Day, have faded into bitter, bewildering disillusion.

Doubtless this cluster of frustrations and disappointments arising from a complex of causes accounts for the dangerously diverting tendency to adopt the simple explanations of wantonness, stupidity or treachery for our predicament. But of course the roots of our difficulties are not in the actions, wise or unwise, of any individual, nor their explanation in such simplicities. Our difficulties are the price of our blessings—the power and pivotal position of our country between East and West in an interval of profound global convulsion.

The fact is that the West is besieged in body and mind; and burning books, abusing scapegoats, assailing straw men—or even Democrats!—will not lift the siege. We cannot insure the security of the Republic by insuring the insecurity of its intelligence. Nor can we cope with our difficulties successfully in absolutes of right or wrong, black or white, or by exploiting the public appetite for simple solutions and prompt and inexpensive results.

To begin let me review some of the major developments that have contributed to the extraordinary drama of our century and to our infinite difficulties and anxieties, because I believe that there is more real security for Americans in understanding than in H-bombs.

I am not a historian, but I doubt if anyone will dispute the incomparably dramatic qualities of the twentieth century. It began with the horse-and-buggy Victorian security of an orderly world in nice balance. Now at mid-century what do we see? In fifty years, distance has been obliterated by a technological revolution that has brought all mankind cheek to jowl, and that has released the creative and obliterative power of the atom. The Golden Age is outside the door but inside all is anxiety and turmoil. Political revolution has shattered the map and created many new fragments of sovereignty. National independence and democracy have scored spectacular victories and suffered shocking defeats. The center of gravity, the power and influence, in world affairs, after moving slowly west from the Tigris and Euphrates valleys, the Fertile Crescent of the Near East, to Egypt, Greece, Rome, Paris and London, has suddenly split and jumped westward clear across the Atlantic to the Western Hemisphere and Washington, and eastward clear across Europe to Moscow on the doorstep of Asia. Two new colossi, the United States and the Soviet Union, have suddenly emerged. Ideas, on which the West has had an export monopoly for centuries, are now also flowing out of the East and colliding everywhere with our Western ideas.

America's rise to world power in the past fifty years is one of the great realities of this epoch. The final conquest of our rich, protected continent; our sudden change from a debtor to a creditor position; and, finally, our emergence from the war physically unscathed as the mightiest military and industrial power and the richest nation on a shattered globe—all this is familiar. But we should also bear in mind something even more important than these physical facts, namely, that our political institutions have matured around the idea of popular consent as the only valid basis of government and of political power. This heretical notion that government derives its just powers from the consent of the governed, we have come to take for granted as the only tolerable way of organized living.

These historically recent concepts of authority springing from the people, of consent, of republicanism, of
democracy and human freedom, have had great vogue
in the Western World of late and stirred the imaginations
and aspirations of people everywhere. Woodrow Wilson
talked of "making the world safe for democracy," and of
"self-determination." New democracies sprouted out of
the ashes of imperial Germany and Austria-Hungary after
the first war, and the revolutionary Western ideas of
government by consent, of individual dignity and freedom, have had massive impact throughout the world.
But it is also well to recall that even some of our native-
born Western brethren, notably the Italians under Mus-
solini and the Germans under Hitler, lapsed into tyranny
and violence to solve their problems. And it is well to
recall, too, that the Western ideas which we have so
long taken for granted have not been universally accepted
and are now brutally beleaguered.

At the same time that the United States was spreading across this continent and Europeans, English, Scotch
and Irish were flowing to us and into the new empires
beyond the seas, the Muscovite Russians were pressing
outward in all directions—to the Arctic, to the Baltic, to
the Black Sea and eastward to the Pacific. They even
crossed the straits to Alaska and down the coast of
California. It was their presence on the then distant
Pacific coast which prompted President Monroe to

issue his famous doctrine; and it was only a long life-
time ago, 85 years, that a reluctant Congress finally
agreed to put up some $7 million to purchase Alaska
and get the Russians out of this hemisphere. "Seward's
Folly," it was called, and there appears to have been little
concern in America at that time for the implications of
Russia's rapid growth. (In fact, some historians suggest
that the Czar's envoy even had to bribe members of
Congress to get the appropriation bill passed. Evidently
Russian subversion is nothing new!)

But there were some who foresaw Russia's might and a
collision with the United States as each filled out a continent, developed its resources, and rose to intercon-
tinental power. In 1865 Lord Palmerston wrote: "As to
Russia, she will in due time become a power almost as
great as the old Roman Empire."

That acute observer, Alexis de Tocqueville, the French-
man, as early as 1835, writes of America and Russia:

> The principal instrument of the former is freedom, of
> the latter slavery. Their points of departure are different,
> they follow different paths. Nonetheless, each of them
> seems intended through some secret design of Providence
> to hold in its hands the destinies of half the world.

And our own Henry Adams at the turn of the century
reflected apprehensively and prophetically lest "the vast
force of inertia known as China was to be united with

the huge bulk of Russia in a single mass which no amount of new force could henceforth deflect."

So we have not been without warning of a collision with Russian imperialism that has come to many Americans all the same as a rude, incomprehensible shock, and that is not explained but only aggravated by communism.

One aspect of Czarist Russian expansion, coinciding in time with ours, is worth noting because it doubtless contributes to the Russian attitude today as it did yesterday and will tomorrow. In the vast areas encompassed by the Russian state there is a lack of natural defenses. Anxiety about the security of its borders is hardly surprising in view of Russia's geography and a history of five invasions from the West since 1610, not to mention the defeat in the East in the Russo-Japanese War. While Russia has lived in a state of insecurity for centuries and was invaded and devastated by Hitler's armies as recently as 1941, it is only now with the development of the long-range bomber and the guided missile that the United States is experiencing for the first time the sensation of vulnerability.

Also the Russian state which commenced and grew from a centralized absolutism did not follow the Western pattern and evolve from autocracy to democracy. Instead the Bolshevik conspiracy that quickly smothered the beginnings of government by consent and captured the democratic revolution of 1917 was but a new expression of absolutism. So Russia remains a fortress of ever more inscrutable, centralized and ruthless despotism. And, as George Kennan has pointed out, "the pursuit of unlimited authority domestically" has compelled the Soviet state to develop what Stalin called "the organs of suppression" to a degree hitherto unknown. Soviet control has, therefore, never been submitted to the test of popular consent because no one fears conspiracy as much as a conspirator.

This, again, is the exact antithesis of the American experience. Here the idea of government, power and policy based on consent has evolved through successive stages of expanding public participation in the processes of popular government; the slaves have been emancipated and enfranchised; property qualifications for voting have been all but abolished; the suffrage has been extended to women; and now we are seriously considering reducing the voting age to eighteen and enfranchising the District of Columbia. Meanwhile we devote more and more effort and money to enlarge participation in public affairs and in the electoral process. Nonpartisan "get out the vote" campaigns are commonplace and we have political action and education groups of all kinds.

In Russia, on the contrary, even the tentative, experimental compromises with absolutism after the rebellion of 1905 have been replaced by the Soviets' reliance on force, thought control, compulsory conformity and the one-party system.

A third difference in the evolution and attitude of Russia and America also deserves mention. Starting east of the Alleghenies the United States rapidly consolidated its continental territory by acquiring large areas by purchase—Florida, the Louisiana Purchase and the Gadsden Purchase. We also fought what looked to some like a war of aggression in Mexico. (Lincoln is reputed to have remarked that the Mexican War reminded him of the Illinois farmer who said: "I ain't greedy 'bout land. I only want what jines mine.") We even experimented with imperialism in Puerto Rico and the Philippines, and promptly salved an uneasy conscience by pouring vast sums into them, not for exploitation but improvement, and then by giving or offering them independence. And it must be added that since the war we have obtained the right to maintain armed forces in West Germany and Japan, traditional threats to Russia, and have built air bases encircling the Soviet Union from Greenland to Saudi Arabia. While these are defensive steps we must expect charges of imperialism from the Communists and not be surprised or indignant if even friendly countries are anxiously mindful that what is defensive can also be offensive.

Yet, aside from the consolidation of the continental land mass at the expense of the aboriginal Indians or by purchase and more recent defensive precautions, the United States has, I think it fair to say, disclosed little expansionist tendency. In fact, both in preaching and practicing the doctrine of self-determination and independence, the sincerity and vigor of our anti-imperialism have been discomforting to some of our colonial allies and embarrassed our relations with our brethren in the democratic faith.

Meanwhile Russia has been consolidating her vast continental land mass, one sixth of the earth's surface, and, in the process, gobbling up all manner of peoples linguistically and ethnically unrelated. For generations Russia has been warring with the Turks and pressing relentlessly but vainly toward the Dardanelles and the Mediterranean. Latterly, however, the Soviet Union has swallowed up her Baltic neighbors Lithuania, Latvia, and Estonia, and recovered territories in the Ukraine and White Russia wrenched away from the Muscovite Czars by the West in the thirteenth and fourteenth centuries. And since the war, of course, the Soviet Union has occupied and subjugated all of Eastern Europe from the Baltic to the Black Sea and recovered rights and real estate in Asia lost in the Russo-Japanese War.

To the great force of this centrifugal outward thrust which is rooted in the distant past of a messianic "Holy Russia" the modern Russians have added a new and potent weapon of imperialism. Communism is the enemy of all antecedent and different systems, and its votaries insist that its destiny is universal triumph over all other systems. Its fundamental philosophical conflict with democracy and the Western humanist tradition is familiar. Repetition would only serve to point out how communism has further accentuated the profound differences between Russia and the United States, politically, geographically, historically and philosophically, differences which long preceded the advent of communism.

So, born in violence and nurtured in fear, despotism and relentless expansion, Russia, already armed with the military weapons of the West, is now armed with this still more dangerous weapon of imperialist aggression. Communism "originated as a product of uneasy Western consciences," to use Dr. Arnold Toynbee's words, and now these Western weapons in Russian hands have been turned against us. Thus at the mid-point of this incredible century the West faces the most serious challenge of modern history.

In addition to the emergence of the United States and the Soviet Union as the major centers of power, with other nations polarized around them or trying to keep

out of either magnetic field of attraction—trying to keep
neutral—this new and uncomfortable position of the
West constitutes one of the dramatic developments of
our times, a development it is not easy for us to comprehend because it is so new for us. But it is not new historically. The West was besieged in the early Middle
Ages for about 300 years by the Arabs from the south.
Then the Mongol flood from the east swept all the way
to the Carpathian slopes. Later the Ottoman Turks
overran southern Europe and pressed up the Danube
valley for three centuries.

But since the Turks fell back from the walls of Vienna
in 1683, Europe has not been on the defensive. Indeed
for more than 250 years the West has been on the offensive, a posture we have long taken for granted. First came
the Crusades, then the voyages of discovery more than
400 years ago, followed by the missionaries, the conquerors, the traders and the colonizers. Europeans seized
and occupied the great Western hemisphere; they divided
up much of Africa and many Africans were shipped to
America as slaves. In the crowded lands of Asia they will
remind you that Europeans occupied the vacant areas
like Australia and New Zealand; that the Dutch empire
in the East Indies stretched across 3,000 miles of Asia;
that Britain's Asian empire numbered a quarter of all
mankind; and that during the past century everyone

punched profitable holes in the soft seaward side of China. Also, as we have seen, Russia has been invaded five times by Western armies since 1610. Moreover, Western aggression was not confined to distant lands and other peoples. Westerners even aggressed against one another. Since the Napoleonic Wars, Germany has attacked its neighbors three times and precipitated much of the misery as well as the power imbalance and dislocation which now afflict the world. In short, it was Western failures that first introduced modern totalitarianism, Fascism and Nazism, to the West; and it was Western jealousy and disunity that opened Europe's door to the Soviet Union for the first time.

From even such a quick review of Western expansion and aggression we should not be surprised and hurt that most of the non-Western majority of the world finds the West guilty of aggression as charged in the Communist indictment, or that on history's long record the West may look as untrustworthy to the Russians as they do to us. And we must likewise expect that some sensitive Asians will view our outrage over Communist aggressions as a little hypocritical. Nor should it be hard for us to understand why so much of the illiterate population of Indo-China has found it so hard to believe that their long-time colonial masters, the French, are fighting Indo-Chinese for Indo-China's independence.

But the chapter of Western offense and ascendancy

ended abruptly with the last war at the mid-century point and the community of Western nations and Western ideas, wherever they have taken root, is now beset more perilously than it ever was before by Arabs, Mongols or Turks—more perilously beset because of the technological revolution of this century and because of the new ideological weapon of communism, which we know is effectively used to exploit grievance, discontent, poverty, nationalism and racism everywhere, and especially among the uncommitted or neutral peoples whose allegiance could tip the scales of power decisively.

The technological revolution, another phenomenon of this strange era, has made our geographies obsolete and also many of our concepts of power and warfare. As the Western United States opened up a hundred years ago, county seats were located roughly in the center of the county so as to be no more than a day's journey by horse from the county limits. Now in the air age the whole United States is no larger than a county fifty years ago or indeed, no larger than a Greek state 500 years before Christ. You can get to Washington in a day's journey from anywhere. Oceans and continents have shriveled, and even wars, as in Korea, are conducted thousands of miles from the combatants' home bases. We are all standing shoulder to shoulder—with a hydrogen bomb ticking in our pockets.

In the past we have seen the small Greek city-states submerged in the Roman Empire, the medieval city-states enveloped by the European nation-states, and the nation-states grow larger and stronger under the whip of technological development. Where political unity and hence effective power have lagged behind the procession, the result has usually been subjugation and disaster for the laggards. During the period of Western ascendancy and rapid technological development from horse to steam, to electricity and internal combustion, and all the related military developments, we have seen the number of separate sovereignties shrink and the power bases in the world get fewer and bigger. The German principalities united; Austria-Hungary gathered separate entities under a single scepter; Italy united, tardily. Even today the sun never sets on Britain's Commonwealth and overseas empire. Preserving a balance between these larger, fewer units of power has been the principal function of diplomacy since Napoleon.

Now, with the destruction of the two wars, the collapse of empire, and the development of jet propulsion and the new weapons, the great nations of Western Europe have shrunk in stature, and power, real and relative, has further concentrated in the superstates of Russia and the United States. But at the same time a large number of separate independent states have emerged from the ashes of empire, mostly in Asia, where the new rulers of China, the Eastern partner of the new Moscow-Peiping axis, are probably dreaming the old dreams of empire like their Soviet colleagues.

Let us look for a moment at this sudden redistribution of sovereignty which is a further remarkable development of the twentieth century and which has nothing to do with communism. In a generation more than 40 million Egyptians and Arabs, some six states, have attained independence. In a few years 570 million Indians, Pakistanis, Ceylonese, Burmese, Indonesians, Israelis, Filipinos and South Koreans, eight more nations, have attained their sovereignty and stepped onto the world's stage. Twenty-five million more Vietnamese, Laotians and Cambodians are in transition. In all some seventeen sovereignties, more than 635 million people, are free and independent of foreign masters or are on the way. And now all Africa is restive in the twilight of colonialism and the dawn of universal independence. Freedom, in short, has served to divide its followers and multiplied the parties, flags, tariffs, currencies, armies, ambitions and voices that bedevil the world.

In Eastern Europe the process has been reversed. Ten states from the Baltic to the Black Sea—about 85 million people—have lost their independence and been enveloped by force in the Soviet power complex. And

China, too, the largest country and culture of all, has gone Communist and has spread the siege of the new imperialism to the borders of all Asia. To the more than 8½ million square miles and 200 million inhabitants of the Soviet Union, 4 million square miles of China and 450 million Chinese have been added to the Communist domain. And we could also add Tibet and North Korea to fill out the enormous land base of Communist power that now extends from central Europe to southeast Asia, from Prague to Canton, from the Baltic Sea to the South China Sea.

On balance, therefore, there has been both an unparalleled growth and an unparalleled decline of national freedom in this century. But what of individual freedom and democratic government? What reinforcements or losses have all this new freedom and the transformed map brought to the beleaguered West's concept of popular consent as man's only tolerable way of life?

In Europe the gains have been substantial. Our adversaries in the last war, Italy and Western Germany, have repudiated their Fascist and Nazi antidemocratic heresies. Greece, formerly a dictatorship, is democratic again, and the only vestiges of the authoritarianism of the 1930's are Spain, Portugal and Yugoslavia. In the Near East, Israel is a genuine and vital democracy, and the triumph of the democratic constitutional spirit in

Turkey is one of the miracles of our age. Elsewhere in the Near East democratic mechanisms command universal lip service and increasing genuine experimentation. In Latin America the struggle goes on, even if the progress is uneven. While only a few of the countries can be called truly democratic, their institutions and the hopes of their people reflect democratic aspirations.

But in Asia the advance in the direction of popular government is spectacular in fact and the more so because there was so little of democratic tradition. India, Pakistan and Ceylon—almost 450 million people—have joined the democratic ranks in the last few years. Burma, another former British domain, after many rebellions and troubles, is also on the way to greater stability and democratic government. Colonialism and the exploitation of subject peoples have always been repugnant to Americans and they are now. But while British imperialism has many sins on its conscience, we should not deprecate its many virtues, one of which is British education in the democratic tradition, or its many achievements, one of which is the successful preparation of colonial peoples for democratic self-government.

In addition to these former British areas, the Philippines is a going democratic concern in which the government changed leadership last year in a peaceful and honest election. Indonesia, with little preparation for self-government and many difficulties, also has hopes of building on a democratic foundation. And in Japan the old authoritarian system has given way to something still in transition but resembling much more a modern constitutional democracy.

If a box score was possible we might balance the loss of the 470 millions of China and North Korea with the addition of the 635 million to democracy's ranks among the Asian countries I have mentioned. And if our definition of "democracy" was even more elastic we might add another 58 million in South Korea, Formosa and Indo-China, raising our total of reinforcements to almost 700 million.

But numbers are misleading and the really important question is whether these nations, new or old, can preserve their newly-won political independence. There will be no chance for government by consent, for democracy and individual freedom, if the fragile newcomers or enfeebled older members of the family of independent nations fall victim by force or guile to the siege of the new Communist imperialism. More and weaker nations do not make for greater strength and resistance. If the lesson of history is that only the strong can be free and the weak must unite or perish, then it is well to remember, as I have said, that the postwar development is disunity, fragmentation of the map and the subdivision of power.

Blood brothers have even divided the Indian continent into a Hindu India and a Moslem Pakistan to the misfortune of both. And both have within them dangerous seeds of further subdivision.

I have tried to suggest some of the dramatic changes of this century that lie behind and beneath the present: the sudden rise to world power of the United States and the Soviet Union from totally different origins, national experiences and basic principles; the technological and political revolutions that have shrunk the world and multiplied the number of states that have a voice in our destiny; and the defensive posture of the West for the first time in 250 years.

We may have been slow to appreciate these massive changes of the twentieth century and their full impact may yet be imperfectly perceived. But the events immediately following the last war are fresh and clear. In China, with the defeat of Japan, Mao Tse-tung exploited the wartime confusion and weakness and the inadequacy of Chiang Kai-shek's government and the Kuomintang party; the military initiative quickly passed to the Communist peasant army, and in a few short years the vastly larger Nationalist forces melted like the snows and all China was a Communist state. The re-creation of China as a great power has come to pass after more than a century of impotence, but under quite different management than we intended.

In Europe the Russian armies advanced on the heels of the retreating Germans into Eastern Europe, from the Baltic to the Black Sea, and settled down to stay, yes, and to attempt to press on to the Eastern Mediterranean and the Czars' long-time goal. Western Europe and Britain were enfeebled, exhausted and impoverished by the gigantic exertion of two wars in rapid succession. The Communists, who had been so active in the resistance movements in the occupied areas, were well organized, aggressive and ready. They moved quickly into positions of influence and power in the countries that had been occupied by the Nazis. We forget that the Vice Premier of liberated France in 1947 was a Communist.

And here in the United States, comforted by our assumed monopoly of atomic weapons and reassured by excessive reliance on the infant United Nations, we quickly demobilized and reverted to the ways of peace and of our past. But the illusion of security and normalcy was short-lived. And we were soon confronted with the fact that our problems had not been resolved by the defeat of Germany and Japan. Instead new vacuums of power had created new difficulties. Russia's cynical violation of its agreements in Eastern Europe and its pressure on Greece and Turkey posed new threats to security.

The concept of great power harmony underlying the United Nations proved an illusion. In short, it became apparent that Russian power could no longer be balanced, or Russian expansion contained, without the active participation and leadership of the United States. There was no longer anyone to do the job for us.

Sixty years ago Lord Bryce wrote of America:

> Safe from attack, safe even from menace, she hears from afar the warring cries of European nations and faiths. For the present at least—it may not always be so—America sails upon a summer sea.

Well, it was no longer so.

Never before, I dare say, have a government and a people had to learn so much so quickly. That we did face the realities decisively and in time may have changed the course of history.

The year 1846 was one of decision for the United States—the decision to fill out its continental position and thereby to become a great power in the world.

The year 1947 was another year of decision for the United States—the decision to shoulder the burdens of a great power in the world.

I suppose the historians will pay increasing attention to 1947. In that year, after two years of futile peace negotiations with the Russians, General George Marshall, as our new Secretary of State, faced the fact that negotiation without power was futile and that the United States and its allies were almost powerless. Since the war the United States Army in Europe had dropped from 3,500,000 to two divisions with no more than six ready battalions in reserve at home. The British and the French, with large overseas commitments, were similarly enfeebled, while the Russians had forty combat divisions in Europe and a hundred in reserve. Moreover, the economic deterioration was, if anything, worse. Even food was desperately short. Bread rations in France and Italy fell to half a pound a day that autumn.

Confronted with implacable malice, the menacing preponderance of Soviet strength, and the futility of further negotiation from manifest weakness, the warborn alliance with the USSR ended in 1947, and the East and the West divided in open recognition of a state of enmity that still persists. And it was in that year that the United States took the bold initiative with a series of steps designed to save Greece and Turkey and, by restoring economic health and political stability to Europe, to enable the allies to negotiate from strength instead of weakness. The steps initiated in 1947 are within the fresh memory of all of us:

Aid to Greece and Turkey, sorely beset by Soviet threats and Communist guerrillas.

Announcement by President Truman of the policy of assistance to peoples threatened internally or externally and prepared to resist.

The Marshall proposal to arrest the economic anemia and vulnerability and restore the health and strength of Western Europe.

The first steps toward the re-establishment of Germany as an asset instead of a burden on the defensive strength of the West.

The Inter-American Treaty of Reciprocal Assistance, our first permanent alliance, which foreshadowed the North Atlantic Treaty and similar alliances in the Pacific.

(And it was also back in 1947 that the loyalty review system in Federal employment was instituted in response to emerging evidence of subversion.)

These first positive steps to organize and sustain resistance to the spread of communism have been rapidly followed by many others: our successful resistance to the Berlin blockade, the establishment of the Federal Republic of Germany, the defense mobilization, the world-wide economic and military assistance programs, the North Atlantic Treaty Organization, the European Defense Community proposal, the system of Pacific treaties, the bloody war in Korea, aid to Indo-China, and so forth. Together they constitute a mighty and global effort to contain aggression, redress the balance of power, counter

Communist penetration, and build the free world's moral, economic and military vitality to the end that the weak and strong can be independent; can live in peace and each work out its own way of life.

How are we getting along with this appalling undertaking? Out of a job—thanks to the voters—I went to see for myself. Starting from San Francisco in March, 1953, with four companions I traveled for six months around the edges of the Communist empire through Asia, the Middle East and Western Europe. I talked to the Emperor of Japan, the Queen of England, the Pope and to all the kings, presidents and prime ministers along my route. And I also talked to countless diplomats, politicians, journalists, students, soldiers, peasants, porters, and multitudes of new and warmhearted friends. Everywhere I encountered an eagerness to talk and a candor of expression among officials that touched and astonished me —and has heavily taxed my discretion. And often the hospitality made me wonder if my hosts were confused and thought I had been elected President in 1952!

It was a sobering experience. For it is more than a privilege; it is a responsibility to be an American in this changing world. It isn't one world; it is more like three worlds—the Communist world, the allied world and the uncommitted world. By the Communist rulers we are feared and hated; feared possibly more than we fear them; hated because we have frustrated their designs, and hated as only totalitarian orthodoxy hates defiant nonconformity. The allied world looks to us for aid, understanding and sober leadership in building the structure of defense, economic order and well-being, and strengthening the grand coalition, on which the security of all of us depends. The uncommitted world, nervous, argumentative, insecure, preoccupied with difficulties and grievances, wants to remain aloof but looks to us, furtively and suspiciously perhaps, for understanding and friendship.

I came back exhilarated by the successes since the United States in 1947 faced the realities of a sick, tottering world and the Soviet Union's aggressive purposes. The Eastern Mediterranean has been saved. Prostrate Europe has risen from its sick bed and its defenses have been restored. Violent Communist insurrections have failed in the Philippines, Indonesia, Burma and Malaya. The Republic of Korea has been successfully defended. For the first time in history collective security has been made to work in a savage test. The newly independent states are still intact, and since the *coup d'état* in Czechoslovakia, the Soviet Union has not added an inch of territory to its domain.

But I also came back oppressed with the infinity of troubles, large and small, which afflict the world. In most of them the United States is concerned, be it the price of rubber, which is so vital to Indonesia's economy; or the Anglo-Egyptian dispute over the Suez base, which is so vital to Middle East defense; or the interminable war in the steaming rice paddies of Indo-China, which is a gate to all Southeast Asia; or neutralism in India, which is the prime Communist target; or world trade, which is obviously indispensable to the workshop nations like Japan, Germany and Britain, and less obviously, but hardly less indispensable, to the producers of raw materials.

One could go on and on reciting the headaches that plague every continent, every corner and every country of the globe—and always the United States. In the state of Travancore-Cochin on the Malabar coast of India, which has the highest percentage of literacy, the highest percentage of Christians and the highest percentage of Communists in all India, the worried leaders told me that owing to the collapse of the market for coco mats in the United States unemployment in that local industry had increased Communist sympathy. In the Khyber Pass the tribal chieftains solemnly insisted that the United States must see that justice was done to Pakistan in Kashmir. In Cyprus I was deluged with pleas for United States support for union with Greece. And so it went right around the world.

Just being an American nowadays is not always comfortable. In the sensitive new areas some will denounce American aid as imperialism; but if it is not forthcoming we are denounced for indifference or discrimination. And sometimes if we stand correctly aloof from the local political scene we are accused of supporting reaction and the status quo. But if we don't keep our hands off and indicate some preference for policies or politicians then we are denounced for interfering. We are damned if we do and damned if we don't—at least now and then.

And there is much misunderstanding and many misconceptions about us, just as one of our major hazards is the strange and distorted pictures we have of others. The neutrals don't fully understand our impatience with neutrality in view of our own long history of neutrality and noninvolvement. Nor do all our friends, who share our view about communism, share our views about Communists. I recall the anti-Communist Catholic youth delegation that called on me in France and left a friend outside in their car because he was a Communist. And peoples who have lived for centuries in perpetual insecurity among predatory neighbors don't understand how there can be such insecurity and fear in America, which has never even been bombed, let alone occupied by an enemy. "McCarthyism," conformity and demagoguery are equated with the Communist and Fascist methods they know and despise. And, of course, there are misconceptions about our militarism, materialism and bottomless wealth; and suspicion that we are less concerned with helping others than helping ourselves. In some quarters there is a feeling that the United States is impulsive, reckless and unreliable, that we are embittered and divided at home, and that domestic political influences may carry more weight in our decisions than America's partners do. In many places there is little understanding of the burden of suffering and expense Americans have borne in recent years in the common cause, or of the social reforms in this country during the past twenty years. Too often the impression is of a rich, reactionary unreconstructed nineteenth century country. Ignorance, propaganda and our own behavior discolor and distort the vision of America.

The list of misconceptions, diligently cultivated by Communist propaganda and often confirmed by our loud, arrogant voices, is long. While the misunderstanding is often irritating it is not incomprehensible, and on the whole it is more than balanced by admiration and gratitude for our faith and fortitude and for our persistence in a monumental effort embracing everything from money, men and machines for defense to malaria control and education of large numbers of students. Here again the illustrations of an awareness of the sincerity of our motives and the magnitude of the effort could be multiplied.

But enough of these familiar facts of mass information and misinformation about one another in this era of mass communication. I came back persuaded that America would stand or fall not just by the tangibles, but by the intangibles of American power and character. And one of them is the effect of words, utterances, language on ourselves and on others.

As Americans we are accustomed to political bad manners and billingsgate. After a century and a half we have developed some immunity to vilification, abuse and misrepresentation in our domestic public dialogue. If not an ornament to the American tradition it is at least a part of it, and we have learned somehow to give it a rough evaluation and get along surprisingly well in spite of deceit, demagoguery and verbal violence. While rough-and-tumble American political manners have been an interesting curiosity to foreigners for generations, they have had little effect on the rest of the world.

But now the situation has changed with the change in America's position in the world. Everyone is listening attentively to what we say but without even our imperfect capacity to evaluate its significance. The voice of America is not just the government radio but the angry words, defiant proclamations and oratorical attitudes of American politicians and leaders. They may be talking to the folks back home for votes or effect, but what they say echoes and re-echoes around the world. And I can personally testify that what they say is often greeted in deadly seriousness as a reflection of America.

The opinions of America are formed from the composite of the voices of America, official and unofficial, true and false. Listening to the hot words, the wild accusations, the bad history, the policy contradictions and plain nonsense on our daily menu dished up for domestic consumption, it is small wonder that the image of America is not always distinct or that the bright vision of the land of the free and the home of the brave is sometimes obscure. We do not realize what injury heedless words and bad manners can do us abroad when the world is all on the same wave length and everyone is listening. To see ourselves as others see us, we must hear ourselves as others hear us. For, in the words of the Apostle: "if the trumpet give an uncertain sound, who shall prepare himself to the battle?"

But there is still another danger in loud, loose tongues. We not only confuse and mislead foreigners but we can mislead and deceive ourselves; we can become the victims of our own propaganda, especially in times of tension and impatience. When passions run high they can also run away. I recall the engaging remark of the French revolutionary who ran to the window muttering: "The mob is in the street. I must see which way they are going, for I am their leader."

Unaccustomed as we are to moderate speech, our petulance, temper or partisanship can have its effect on us as well as the foreigner, especially when it is cloaked in the garments of righteousness and impatience with any solutions that do not promise quick returns. We must be on our guard against the danger to our own people, as well as to our friends, of confusing pronouncements with reality and proclamations with policy. For these are ingredients of extremist opinion. And in these days when moderation and reason are so often equated with appeasement or even disloyalty, we must be careful lest unreason and extremism not only frighten and alienate our friends and fan the flames of neutralism in the world but also mislead the American people.

Looking back to the clamor about the unpopular Jay Treaty in 1795 and John Adams' courageous resistance of the loud demands for war with France a few years later, our history reveals many instances where aroused and articulate public opinion has made wise executive policy more difficult. There is no doubt, for example, that the Kellogg-Briand Pact, now a monument to illusion, was a creation of the force of unrealistic opinion rather than official judgment. And there is little doubt that hostile public opinion delayed repeal of the Neutrality Act and other desirable steps between the outbreak of the last war in 1939 and the attack on Pearl Harbor in 1941.

More recently Korea may have some value as an illustration of what I mean. We intervened there not to unite Korea by force but to resist the Communist attempt to unite Korea by force. When in the fall of 1951 we had repelled the invasion and driven the crumbling North Korean army beyond the 38th parallel, the Indian government warned us of the danger of further advances. A few wise counselors in our own government also anticipated the Chinese reaction if we approached the Yalu River. China's intervention and two years of war may well have been the price for rejecting that advice. How much did the pressure of vocal, articulate public opinion influence the decision? I don't know. But I do know that in our system public opinion is our sovereign; its temperance or caprice is the Republic's shield or hazard. It is easier to light fires than to extinguish them, and passion and extremism are dangerous leaders.

If public opinion is our sovereign in this people's government, then the enlightenment and maturity of our public opinion about this troubled world pose vast difficulties for us in competition with dictators uninhibited by the public's myriad voices, wise and foolish, thoughtful and heedless.

The culmination of the ordeal of the twentieth century, then, is a world in which power has concentrated more closely and, conversely, the weakness of disunion has been spread more widely by nationalism and independence. And this world is sharply divided. It has fallen to America's lot to organize and lead that portion of the world which adheres to the principle of consent in the ordering of human affairs against its first attack in several hundred years. It is an assignment we undertook not by choice but by necessity and without prior experience. The burden is without historical parallel and so is the danger, and so is our response. The first phase is ending. The outward thrust of aggression in Europe has been arrested. And now we shall have to address ourselves to Asia, to perpetual siege and to the unending tasks of greatness. For the quest for peace and security is not a day's or a decade's work. For us it may be everlasting.

Edmund Burke said that "We can never walk surely but by being sensible of our blindness." As we enter the second half of this century of crisis, the next but probably not the last era of decision between consent and compulsion, a consciousness of the limits of our wisdom is our best companion because it is the root of responsibility. And freedom is the reward of responsibility. We will have to learn to think of our responsibilities not as a passing annoyance but as a status in an interdependent world that we Americans must live in, work in and pray for in the accents of humility and faith in a power greater than ours, our enemies' or any man's.

Perpetual Peril

I HAVE attempted to uncover some of the roots and origins of the difficulties and perils of this troubled age, and some of the steps that have been taken to set things right. We have looked backward a bit to the near and distant past. Now let us look for a moment at the fresher events of yesterday and today; let us take a little inventory of the present.

The tense scene at mid-century seems to me to be dominated by two immense facts. The first is the revolution of rising expectations and the new political independence of masses of awakening peoples. From West Africa to Indonesia millions of human beings are now emerging from foreign domination and fiercely demanding relief from hunger, pestilence and oppression. The second is the constant overhanging threat of aggressive communism to national independence and to our concepts of political freedom and individualism which we have taken for granted for so long.

Our attention in America and the attention of the Western World has been largely focused on the second of these facts—the Communist challenge and, more narrowly, on Russia. But the attention of the peoples in revolution has not. Preoccupied with their own ferment and anti-Western revolutionary tradition, they have not measured the Communist threat to their tender independence in our dimensions of time or magnitude.

The postwar behavior of the Soviet Union has outraged and angered us in the West—in part, I suppose, because of the illusory hopes built up during the warborn alliance and because of our own idealistic and moralistic dogmas of international behavior. Nations—especially recent allies—are supposed to leave one another alone, to live and let live. It was in defense of this simple, sensible and moral principle of international conduct that, in association with Russia, we administered a terrible licking to Germany and Japan. Yet to our shocked surprise, almost before we had ceased to fight and denounce our common enemies, the Nazis and the "Japs," the treacherous Russian bear, our comrade in arms, rose up to bite the hand that fed it, to prey upon the enfeebled victims of war, to try to subjugate friend and foe alike by a noxious design of conquest through coercion or subversion.

Perhaps we had no right to be surprised. Some of the farthest-seeing men who had studied the Russians at close hand—men like George Kennan and Averell Harriman— had cautioned us against these illusions. Others among us raised warning flags very early. I, myself, if I may insert an immodest self-quotation, said in March of 1946 to an audience in Chicago that "We must forsake any hope that [the Soviet Union] is going to lie still and lick her awful wounds. She's not. . . . She intends to advance her aims, many of them objectives of the Czars, to the utmost." Nevertheless, justified or not, surprised we were, and our surprise became outrage, horror, and fear, as the Kremlin's dread design of world dominion became more naked and more grasping, as blow after blow of the iron fist smashed at liberty in Europe, in the Middle East, in Asia.

Today there can be no more surprises about the nature of Communist imperialism, about its cynical ambitions, about its use of every means from military aggression to Trojan horse tactics of fifth columns and internal subversion in every country in the world. But today, it seems to me, we are overinclined to let outrage and fear—bad masters—influence our response to events consistently conforming with this ruthless, implacable pattern; and we have certainly let the exploiters of fear and moral indignation reach dangerous heights of public influence in our country.

Today, furthermore, we have became so fascinated by the evil conspiracy directed from Moscow that we tend to overlook the massive problems that stare down on us elsewhere. By no means all of our troubles are due to communism or Russia, and we must take care not to oversimplify or underestimate the complexity and dimensions of our responsibility by attributing all the difficulties of the present to communism and to failure to solve the Communist threat. We were overborne and almost drowned by the torrent of wishful thinking after the war—what D. W. Brogan has termed "the illusion of American omnipotence." We have not yet recovered our sanity or balance from the shock of dismay that China didn't turn out as we expected, that friends became enemies and enemies friends, and that our power and influence to arrange things according to our own liking turned out to be limited. There may be further surprises and disappointments, and they are the more likely if we do not understand the limits of our own strength and if our preoccupation with the Communist menace is too exclusive. For, after all, communism is not the only cause even of the Russian problem. On the record of history, an industrialized Russia would very likely be expansionist if Czars instead of commissars sat in the Kremlin; and as for Asia and Africa, inexorable changes would be taking place there if Marx's *Kapital* was a forgotten book in the dusty recesses of our libraries.

The fact is that even if Russia did not exist, even if Karl Marx had never been born and if there were no Communist parties or sympathizers, a multitude of problems would still bedevil the world. I shall mention only some of them. In Europe, thanks to American assistance, economic recovery from the war has been spectacular; but, now that economic aid is ending, Europeans are anxiously seeking the expanding foreign trade that must support them in the future. In the Near East, insurgent nationalism has resulted in the eviction of the British from Iran, the dispute with Egypt over the great military base that stretches for 100 miles along the Suez Canal, and the cold bitterness of Arab-Israel relations that seem no better five years after the armistice in their shooting war. In Asia, Japan has lost its empire, its sources of raw materials and also many of its nearby markets owing in part to bitter memories of wartime occupation as well as the passion for economic self-sufficiency in formerly dependent areas. In Malaya, fighting the Communist terrorists in the jungles is not Britain's only task. There is also the riddle of how to prepare the country for independence and self-government when there are as many Chinese as Malays. Indonesia is demanding Irian, the western portion of New Guinea; India and Pakistan after five years have not yet agreed on even the method of settlement of the long standing and dangerous dispute about the future allegiance of the great province of Kashmir.

And looming over all these immediate points of friction and danger is the massive fact of the suddenly unchained aspirations of hundreds of millions of people in the Near East, Asia and Africa. Independence and self-government have come to most of these people in a recent blinding rush. They have not yet solved the tremendous problems of poverty, illiteracy, administrative inexperience, economic underdevelopment, political instability and decaying feudalism. Restless millions live barely above the starvation line, and, fast as they increase their output of food, their populations are growing faster with the spectacular success of disease control and public health programs.

Is it any wonder that much of the non-Communist world is more preoccupied with its own affairs than with the menace of international communism? Is it any wonder that, conscious as its leaders are of Soviet expansion in Europe and the Communist conquest of China, they are also mindful of their hard-won independence from their former colonial masters and that large fragments of the world are still under the domination of what they regard as Western imperialism?

We will be hearing about nationalism, a Western product, for a long time to come and in more places than

Indo-China. The explosive forces of nationalism, anti-colonialism and independence, which we in America, the first modern product of anticolonial revolution, should understand very well, were not invented by communism. But communism will aggravate them, and exploit them, and gain by them, whenever and wherever it can. And we in the United States will have to learn to expect such exploitation of natural forces to which slogans like "massive retaliation" are no answer and nuclear intimidation no solution.

In short the Western message of independence has reverberated around the world—with results sometimes disconcerting to us of the West. And so has the message of Western technology—the message of a technology which has shattered time and distance and released sources of energy beyond our comprehension—the message which means unmistakably that poverty, hunger, disease and servitude are not the immutable destiny of the long-suffering two-thirds of the human race who are largely colored. This revolution of rising expectations, this awareness that there can be relief and improvement, this insistence that science and engineering must have the answers, and quickly, is a product not of communism but of our own industrial revolution and material progress.

In the underdeveloped areas the people know about the great contrast in productivity between their non-

industrialized nations and the Western nations, especially
the fabulous United States. They are mostly illiterate,
they read no newspapers, they hear no radios, but the
word has traveled, they have heard, they know. And they
too want to industrialize, to use their raw materials for
their own enjoyment, and to create jobs for the many
unemployed or underemployed in their overcrowded,
static, agrarian societies. They want to change a world
which has not changed for centuries; and they want to
make up for lost time.

Is it any wonder that from their standpoint, and to
some of them, the end looks more important than the
means? Is it any wonder that they are impressed by
Russia's dramatic—and well-dramatized—achievements
in industrialization and by the highly colored stories
that are coming out of China? Can they win Operation
Bootstrap by democratic, voluntary methods, or is force
the only answer? This is the underlying issue in a large
area of the world. It is the most important issue of our
time and it is not an easy issue to solve, even in more
fortunate regions, let alone in the heat, the teeming
pressures and the urgency of an Asian capital. And, need-
less to say, it is not an issue that will be resolved merely
by anti-Communist pronouncements or by nervous exclusive emphasis on military defense.

For the Communist conspiracy is eagerly trying to cash

in on all these tensions and troubles, be it the poverty of a factory worker in Turin, anticolonialism in North Africa, political instability in the Middle East, a peasant's credulity in Indo-China or his land hunger in Iran. Communism everywhere seeks to ally itself with this vast revolution as its friend and convert it to its ends. And this is a threat at least as great as the long, red shadow of the military might of the Soviet Union with which we are more familiar.

These, then, are the two elements in our present situation which pose our greatest problems—the menace of Communist aggression in all its forms, and the revolution of rising expectations. And let it be said to our credit that by and large our national policies these last years have been well directed toward meeting exactly these problems. The Marshall Plan and the Point Four program, the military assistance measures and the battle for Korea, these great endeavors of our foreign policy have been attempts to grapple with the real, the actual problems before us.

And now what is our position? After seven years of ceaseless effort, enormous expenditures, burdensome taxes and the loss of many lives, where are we?

I think it can be said, briefly and soberly, that we have survived the major crisis, that an unsteady equilibrium has been established in Europe and, if Indo-China is saved, in Asia as well, but that no settlement or security is in sight and we are now settling down for a long endurance contest. If such an estimate of the present situation is cold comfort, I think we Americans can find great satisfaction in reflecting on what the situation might be had we not made and sustained this great exertion.

And failure would have been so easy. It is little short of a miracle of politics and diplomacy that we have successfully resolved the constant dilemma between the requirements—in military effort, money, political maturity and fortitude—that flow from being the only power strong enough to organize and lead a great coalition of nations, and the costs—economic, political and psychological—of meeting those requirements. This achievement has exacted its price, not only in money and resources, but in interior strain and spiritual anxiety. Yet the fact that it has been sustained so long is heartening evidence, it seems to me, of democracy's will to survive—above all, of democracy's ability to compete with totalitarianism, not just in war but in the more complex tasks of cold war, when we must rely on co-operation and persuasion where the enemy can employ coercion and command.

We have come a long way, but I suspect we also have a longer way to go. Through the conquest of China, communism is striking for dominance in the Far East.

There is a truce but no peace in sight in Korea; Communist armies are attacking harder and harder in Indo-China, and Communist parties are fishing in all the troubled waters of Asia. Europe is divided, and the Berlin Conference left no doubt that Russia intends to maintain its military and political line in Europe, and will exploit every crack in Western unity. It is a reasonable assumption that the Geneva Conference will reveal the same objectives in Asia. In Latin America Communist pressure has been evident in British Guiana and in Guatemala near the Panama Canal. Anticolonialism in Africa is a fertile field for Communist agitation for change. There are even some Communists in North America who seem to command a disproportionate amount of our attention.

In contrast to our behavior after the First World War the United States has made the decision that it cannot retreat into isolation and let the rest of the world slip under the Iron Curtain bit by bit, drawing the cord of strangulation around our own necks tighter and tighter as it goes. So the United States, as the only power great enough to organize and lead the resistance, must be committed to the struggle as long as it lasts. Most of the great sieges of history have lasted a long while. The Greeks and Romans spread their dominion and culture across the known world for almost a thousand years, and the Greek language of the New Testament was understood from the Malabar coast of India to Marseilles. Then Islam, armed with a creed and a passion for reform, rose from the Arabian desert and for almost another thousand years gradually spread out and around the heartland of Christian Europe all the way to the plains of India on the East and to the Atlantic on the West. Even to this day the Moslem religion is dominant in distant Indonesia and deep into Africa and the same written Arabic can be read by Moslems from Morocco to Iran. The Western expansion which followed, with its conquest of the seas and its encirclement of Islam, has been of much shorter duration. And now in our time its course has been reversed, not alone by external enemies, but also by our own internal disunion and by our own Western contributions to world revolution through nationalism and technology.

It would be foolish to suggest that the present expansion of communism is another great historical movement with the durable qualities of its predecessors. On the contrary, it has no basic moral, spiritual or cultural content. Marxian materialism is in fact a cruel denial of humanity's hunger of the heart and spirit; the police state is a brutal rejection of man's inherent love of freedom; and the spread of the Communist discipline is a new and more terrible form of imperialism, deadly to the spirit of national independence. Communism thus runs against the grain of humanity and the aspirations of civilized society, and these are formidable obstacles to its ultimate triumph. Yet, armed with a fanatical faith and a program of dogmatic reform in a time of tension and change, already disposing of vast armies and master of a third of the world, forever seeking new strength and new support in the troubled awakening of the great new continents, it is a force we can underestimate only at the risk of our own destruction.

In short, we live in a time of perpetual peril, and the end is not in sight. I won't attempt to guess whether this is a thirty-year war or a hundred-year war. Nor would it be profitable to speculate on how it will eventually turn out. America will have much to do with that. But one thing is certain: it cannot turn out well if the coalition of Western democracies disintegrates either militarily or ideologically. For there are two struggles— the power struggle and the ideological struggle. Essential to both is the steadfast solidarity of the coalition cemented by the United States in the postwar emergency.

Let us consider for a moment the evolution of the power aspects of the struggle. During the war we all hoped that peace might be assured by a harmony of great power interests growing out of wartime co-operation against the Axis and the need for postwar co-operation in reconstructing the ravaged world. This was the central concept of the Security Council of the United Nations. Acting on our hopes and public pressures, we quickly demobilized. In the presidential campaign of 1944, before the war was even over, the Republican candidate called for the release and return of our forces "at the earliest practical moment after victory." And General Eisenhower later assured us that demobilization had not been too fast and that there was no reason to anticipate any conflict of interest with the Soviet Union—which reminds me with a shudder of Cardinal Richelieu's words: "Give me six sentences written by the most innocent of men and I will hang him with them."

At all events, the illusion of peace through harmony crumbled with the realization that Soviet ambitions were unlimited. So in the fateful year of 1947, as we have seen, we turned to another concept—peace through power.

It was the belief of some that the organization and development of the overwhelming economic and military potential of the non-Communist world, added to our atomic monopoly, would produce an opportunity to negotiate peace through a preponderance of power. There followed a series of pacts, arrangements and programs so extensive that it may now be said that the sun never sets on an American commitment.

But, if the effort was to achieve a clear preponderance of power, it was doomed almost as it began. When the North Atlantic Treaty was signed in April, 1949, the Kremlin was already preparing its first atomic test; and, incidentally, communism was consolidating its hold on China. The concept of peace through a preponderance of power became obsolete as soon as our atomic monopoly was broken. Thereafter it became apparent that either side would have the permanent capability of inflicting grievous damage and destruction on the other. The hope of preponderant power faded away in the ghastly vistas of thermonuclear, supersonic war.

Yet the failure to achieve the results intended does not condemn the results achieved. Thanks to American initiative, tired and tried peoples, especially in Europe, turned chaos into order, weakness into strength. Stalin's plan to add the vital industrial centers of Europe to the Communist system failed. Instead, the economy of Western Europe has been restored and production greatly exceeds prewar levels. More than two million men are under arms and many more stand by in trained reserves. And there has been a steady development of political and economic co-operation, even though Americans seem more disappointed with the delays than cheered by the progress.

In short, if we have not been able to establish a preponderance of power in the West, we have succeeded in establishing a *balance* of power. By that I mean recognition on all sides that revision of the status quo in Europe by threat of force is not possible and that revision by force would provoke world war.

The preservation and extension of this balance, attained at such expense and exertion, appears then to be the first order of business, until we can move on to a satisfactory international system for the limitation and control of military power, and ultimately, let us pray, to the realization of our dream of peace by the concerting of all interests among all nations, great and small.

This concept of a balance of power, it should be emphasized, is not a static thing. Once achieved, it does not become ours forever like the tennis tournament cup. Nor can it be maintained merely by words and wishes. It can only be secured by continued labor and sacrifice. And a balance of power between ourselves and our mortal foe requires not only great military strength on our part but a balanced distribution of that strength—a distribution which would enable us to act in a variety of situations and to respond if need be to a variety of threats.

The retaliatory force of air-atomic power is, in my judgment, an indispensable part of our strategy of defense, just as it has been since the last war. But a program of "massive and instantaneous retaliation" is not enough by itself to preserve the balance of power we have so laboriously achieved. Such capacity did not prevent Korea. Nor did it provide us a means of resolving that bitter struggle. Nor has such talk brought about the solution we desire in Indo-China. Many situations may arise where we will be obliged to bring power to bear to arrest subversion or aggression, but not by means of atomic bombing followed by counterretaliation and world war in which our allies would be the first victims. If, as many say, atom and hydrogen bombs have made total war an obsolete conception, then conventional weapons and forces may well be of more importance than ever in the clouded days ahead. If atomic power is, in a sense, neutralized, then the coalition will need local strength against local aggression more than ever.

As maintaining the coalition and the power equilibrium will require a sustained and balanced military effort, so developing our ideological strength will require a sustained and balanced moral and diplomatic effort; and for that we shall have to clear the air of the fantasies associated with the idea of dictating our terms or philosophy through a preponderant power which doesn't exist.

Diplomacy, for example, is not the art of asserting ever more emphatically that attitudes should not be what they clearly are. It is not the repudiation of actuality, but the recognition of actuality, and the use of actuality to advance our national interests. Take such vexed problems as neutralism or negotiation. Neutralism sometimes provokes heated demands from our leaders that the uncommitted nations sign on our dotted line or else—as if we ourselves had not practiced neutrality for more than a century. Indeed it is well for us to remember that we intervened in the last two world wars only in the nick of time and only after our territory or rights had been directly assailed.

Neutralism is something we must live with, whether we like it or not. No matter how foolish it is, it is far better for us to have countries neutral than to have them join the Communist bloc. And the great danger is not that we have some neutralism but that we may have much more to contend with if we become divided from our friends.

Similarly with negotiation—a word that in some frenetic circles seems to have become a synonym for appeasement. Of course, we must be prepared to negotiate, where negotiation promises advantage. Negotiation is not only the means, however gradual, of settlement with our adversaries; it is also the means of ascertaining our adversaries' terms of settlement. Moreover, at this stage it is even more important in reassuring our apprehensive friends about our peaceful intentions and thereby strengthening our own coalition.

I have said that there are two struggles taking place within this framework created by the aggressions of communism and the awakening of the underdeveloped peoples—the power struggle and the ideological struggle. While it is impossible to separate the two, it may be said, I think, that in the West the struggle has become primarily a power struggle with ideological undertones. In the East, we have, for the time being, the opposite situation, where the main battle is being fought, except in limited areas, in terms of ideas rather than armies. (This may seem to be contradicted by the long power struggle in Indo-China, but it should be remembered that what has become a Communist aggression started and is still largely sustained by Viet-Namese nationalism and anti-colonialism.)

Let us look for a few moments at the West. The division of Europe with all of its implications; the division of Germany, the largest, strongest power in Europe; Anglo-American and Russian forces facing each other in the heart of Europe—all these situations constitute an acute threat to peace. The precarious and uneasy nature of the present balance is revealed by the June, 1953, riots in Berlin and more recently by the disorders which the sudden and ill-fated "solution" provoked in Trieste. And the Berlin Conference made it clear that the Soviet Union will not and the coalition cannot permit an expansion of the other's power in Europe. Even at the risk, indeed the certainty, of higher walls of hatred in Eastern Europe, the Soviet has made it clear again, after an interruption of five years and the death of Stalin, that its objective is a Communist Germany, or at least a susceptible and powerless Germany, and the eviction of Western forces. In other words, its objective is to upset the present balance of power.

I don't know and my guess would be worthless as to the relative weight of the factors of fear and expansionist ambitions in the obdurate attitude of the Soviet. Some will say that Russia fears us as much as we fear them; that they are prisoners of their history and their Communist dogmas about "the crisis of capitalism" and its inevitable ultimate recourse to war. But they are perhaps even more prisoners of their own system of society—a system of tension, held together by calculated fear, in which a committee maintains absolute power at home by invoking a sense of absolute danger from abroad. A society which is unwilling to give its own people a measure of freedom cannot easily risk normal and equable relations with the outside world. Certainly totalitarianism begets a pervasive mood of fear—fear of the world outside, fear of the state, fear of the police, fear of neighbors, fear of one's own innermost thoughts.

And the Soviet leaders can render this fundamental

and calculated fear the more plausible by pointing to events of history. Certainly the repeated invasions of the past, the allied intervention after the first war, Hitler's invasion in the second, the present circle of bomber bases and the military strength of the Western coalition must contribute to Soviet apprehension. Nor can there be any doubt that they regard the presence of American, British and French forces in Germany as a threat, just as we regard the Red Army in Eastern Europe as a threat. There seems to be little point in asserting that because we have no aggressive intentions, the Soviet Union should not fear the alliance of an armed and unified Germany with the West or the liberation of the satellites. To the Kremlin the threat inherent in these allied capabilities for action will not be easily erased with words or even guarantees. And it is difficult to argue that they need not fear the passions which would be released if Soviet forces withdraw from Eastern Europe.

Whether Soviet intransigence is the result of fear or ambition, or both, as is probably the case; whether, indeed, it is inherent in their totalitarian system, it is the view of many with whom I have talked around the world that, now confronted with certain and strong resistance, Soviet military adventure in the West is most unlikely. In one important respect it is fortunate that the adversary in the atomic age is totalitarian Bolshevism rather than totalitarian Nazism. The latter, personified by Hitler and unthinkable without him, was suicidally romantic and naïvely irrational. There is good reason to believe that the Kremlin, with or without Stalin, resembles the bookie more than the gambler. It will calculate the odds. It will take risks but it won't risk everything. It will avoid ventures which might involve ruinous losses even if it has to forgo ventures which might yield large gains. As conservative revolutionaries, somewhat sobered by thirty-five years of power, as compared to Hitler's six short years in 1939, they will also liquidate ventures that prove unprofitable or no longer profitable, as in Greece, the Berlin blockade and Korea.

On such an appraisal of a fearful, cautious, stubborn and implacable adversary, the uneasy, unsatisfactory status quo must be maintained until some solution can be found to the basic problem of a divided Europe, which is a divided Germany. Perhaps in time the mounting tensions of a divided Germany will merge into the larger problem of a divided Europe. Perhaps the Soviet rulers may in time conclude that the withdrawal of British-American forces from a united and really independent Europe is safer and better than maintaining Russian garrisons amid the rising tensions of an unnaturally divided Europe.

We should, I believe, be thinking beyond the cold

confines of the cold war. Perhaps the ultimate solution will be a declaration of independence for all of Europe, based on the developing strength of the organs of European unity. Perhaps there will evolve the concept of an independent united Europe linked with the United States and Britain on the one hand, and the Soviet Union on the other, in mutual security arrangements pledging common resistance against aggression by any one of the three.

But such remote conjectures are less instructive and important for the present than improving the balance of power and the strength and solidarity of Western Europe on which any permanent and better adjustment must depend. For it is obvious that the Soviet will generate and exploit disunity in our coalition, hoping to deal with its adversaries separately, preferably one against the other.

Their objective, of course, is victory without war. And our objective is neither war nor victory, but an opportunity for all to work out their own destiny in their own way in independence and freedom. To accomplish that, military strength to deter or defeat aggression and economic strength to resist aggression by subversion are the first requirements; and the second is a community of interest and purpose among us in order to keep our strength intact and in order to negotiate as one, not as many. The first phase has been accomplished. America returned to Europe not to intrude but to redress the imbalance of strength and arrest the march of communism. Now the second phase, holding the line, maintaining the coalition and negotiating where possible, is upon us.

And here our adversary has opportunities and advantages in the disunity and multiple sovereignties of the non-Communist world. In Europe, under the Soviet shadow Sweden stands aloof, Italy is weak, Germany is divided and disarmed, France is bedeviled from all sides and demoralized, and, for very good reasons, as wary of a restored Germany as of Russia. Britain is steadfast but her first allegiance is to the Commonwealth. And, to pass for a moment beyond Europe, the Middle East, except for the sturdy Turks and alert little Israel, is largely a power vacuum. So is much of Latin America. India is neutral and Japan disarmed and dependent. The free world comprises many nations, cultures, languages and levels of development which have the effect of subdividing collective power and confusing collective purpose. Our focus is not the same. Our coalition speaks with many voices and many tongues. Intracommunity bickering, conflict and mistrust obscure the steady vision of extracommunity danger. And, as we saw in Europe, first in 1914 and again in 1939, a house divided against itself will fall.

I could go on. But the point is that, in contrast with our divisions and imbalances, we dare not overlook the element of strength in the monolithic unity of the Communist world. Maybe the Russians are just gritting their teeth and holding on, waiting for the collapse of Western power and purpose as foretold by their prophets.

Coalitions are nothing new. There have been several successful ones in modern European history. A coalition frustrated the effort of Louis XIV to impose absolutism on Europe. Napoleon was defeated by a coalition, and so were the Kaiser and Hitler. But the members of a coalition have a way of falling apart after the common danger has passed. And that, of course, is all the greater a hazard to a coalition largely of European states as the immediacy of the danger of general war in Europe subsides and the danger shifts to Asia.

Recognizing the improved posture of the West and the changes wrought in these historic, crowded years, Russian policy is changing too. The intimidation of vast armaments, ceaseless and violent propaganda, a hammer blow here and there, are not enough. Now they will stubbornly hang onto every vantage point and use every device to crack up the coalition, to discourage American participation in European affairs, and to diminish and disrupt the European defense effort. Instead of direct political assault, the Communist parties will make parliamentary alliances with left-wing groups in an attempt to recreate the "popular fronts" of earlier days, always with a view to obstruction and frustration. Soft words and conciliatory gestures are in the repertoire too. Already the Russians have relinquished claims to the Straits, extended the olive branch instead of the pistol to Tito, etc. Moscow is busily negotiating barter agreements and courting Western Europe with the device to which it is most susceptible—trade. As commercial pressure grows, the number of takers may grow too, and with it the dependence of non-Communist economies, particularly in Asia. Proposals such as China's agreement with Ceylon to exchange rice at prices under the market for rubber at prices above the market will be difficult for weak economies and governments to resist.

The propaganda line is changing also. Heretofore the United States, for example, was pictured as a predatory imperialist that had come to Europe to stay with malevolent designs on weaker states. Now, when Europe is nervous about American withdrawal, the Communists tell the Europeans that we are fickle and unreliable and will pull out one of these days and leave them to the mercy of a rearmed Germany. Many more students from non-Communist countries, by no means all of them party members, are being invited to study in the Soviet Union and China, and carefully indoctrinated groups of Russian and

Chinese singers, actors, dancers, musicians and athletes are appearing beyond the Iron Curtain.

It should be noted too that the Russian economy may have been expanding at a faster yearly rate of growth than even our own. Already one third the size of ours, it is evidently strong enough now to warrant a change of emphasis to the production and purchase abroad of consumer goods, besides carrying the formidable burden of steadily increasing foreign policy commitments. If the Soviet economy can maintain its present pace of expansion, Russian output may well be from three to four times as great in 1970 as it is today. Should the time come, as some foresee, when the standard of living in the Soviet Union is as good or better than in the democracies of Western Europe, the consequences would be formidable to say the least.

The hazards of internal weakness and instability in many countries have not diminished in recent years. Confronted with a possible loss of cohesion as the immediate danger of general war diminishes, challenged by more resourceful, subtle and flexible exploitation of opportunities by the Soviet, American leadership of the free coalition will face increasingly severe material and moral tests. Certainly any major economic recession here in the United States, which God forbid, would quickly multiply the inherent centrifugal forces of division and

recrimination in the coalition, and lend credence to what
Stalin used to call "the deepening of the general crisis
of capitalism."

Perhaps it is worth a moment to look more closely
at some less obvious factors in Europe—and in Asia as
well—which contribute both to misunderstanding and
hope. Bursts of ill temper and irritation on both sides of
the Atlantic obscure for us the genuine appreciation
abroad of America's saving role. Nor do we probably
appreciate the fact that, with Europe's increasing
strength and self-reliance, our postwar relationship is
breaking up and Europe is asserting its independence
and talking back to us now. We who fought for our independence from Europe should not be surprised when
Europe has a similar recoil from advice, direction and
domination from across the Atlantic. It should be remembered that multitudes of Americans have been busily
mending old Europe's ways with American money and
"know-how" and confidence that our methods are best.
However benevolent the purpose, however desirable the
changes, the reaction was inevitable. It would be the
same here if the tables were reversed and Europeans had
been impressing us with our deficiencies and the superior
merits of their manners, products and way of life. The
excesses of McCarthyism, pronouncements of rigid
policy by American leaders, intemperance and hysterics

of any kind, the growing emphasis on the military aspect of anti-Communist defense, patronizing attitudes and displays of arrogance, wealth and fear, all are exaggerated abroad and summoned as witnesses to prove that America is overbearing and domineering, or erratic and frightened, and not the citadel of freedom, the pattern of perfection and fountain of wisdom after all.

For most Europeans their newspapers, radio and hearsay, and our movies are the source of information about the United States. They know little about us and don't have the same means of evaluating these external impressions of the American scene that we do. That there is much misunderstanding and that we don't look as magnanimous, disinterested and righteous as we do to ourselves is less surprising than the great underlying respect, friendliness and good will.

It seems to me that the rapidly emerging spirit of independence in Europe ("even from its best friends," to use Churchill's phrase), the increasing scrutiny of our policies and critical objectivity about the United States, is wholesome. While it complicates the difficulties of leadership, it will constantly remind us that this is a coalition, a partnership, and the members are not satellites. And certainly we should rejoice that our friends in Europe are not resigned to permanent dependency and henceforth propose to assume a more positive part in the direction of our common concerns.

The European power equilibrium, I have suggested, depends on the maintenance of the coalition; and the coalition, as we have seen, will be pulled this way and that by soft Soviet voices, by resentment of American domination, by healthy aspirations for independence—and also, inevitably, by differing assessments of danger and self-interest.

Where, in all this, does our interest lie? It lies, I believe, in the hope that this emerging self-reliance and spirit may give further momentum to the movement for European unity—a movement which, as it succeeds, will be a factor of incalculable weight in this precariously balanced and dangerously divided world. For separately the enfeebled countries of Western Europe are an invitation to further mistrust and disunion. But together this mighty reservoir of people, skills, industry and culture would be a ponderous weight on the scales.

The dream of a united Europe is as old as the Romans. Conquerors from Charlemagne to Hitler have tried by force and persuasion to hammer or fit the many pieces together again. Countless wars, plans, groupings and blocs wander across the panorama of European history and disappear into thorny thickets of realities. As the center of gravity, power and influence in world affairs ever since Caesar's legions fell slowly back to tottering Rome, there has been little external inducement to arrest the growth of nationalism and separation in Europe. Now in our time the siege from the East and the emergence of the new colossi, Russia and America, are stirring Europe to action, with encouragement from us and interference from beyond the Iron Curtain.

Already the Schuman Plan, a genuine international government for the basic industrial resources of Western Europe, is a going concern. This was a French concept. So also was the European Army which we call the European Defense Community. EDC was born in the emergency. It was a response to Anglo-American insistence on rearming the Germans to shoulder a portion of the defense burden and the French fear of a rearmed, independent Germany. Conceived as a plan to utilize German armed might and still control its use by Germany, which in the past has been more dangerous not only to Europe but to the United States than Russia, the fate of EDC hangs in the balance, as we know. Like the proverbial horse behind the cart, a third project, a constitution for a political community of Europe, has followed, and is under active consideration.

That the progress toward the realization of European union is slow is less of a wonder than that there has been any progress at all, considering the infinite difficulties. The fear of German domination of a military community is echoed in the fear of German economic and

political domination so long as Britain hesitates to sub-
ordinate its ties with the Commonwealth and participate
as part of the new Europe. And there is no minimizing
the thousand and one difficulties in the way of even a
Western European federation—which, of course, is all
that is possible as long as Eastern Europe remains behind
the Iron Curtain. Eastern Europe was the food surplus
and raw materials area, and the union of Western Europe
would be a union of essentially industrial and highly
competitive countries, only two of which, France and
Denmark, can feed themselves and leave anything for
export. To the need for food and raw materials must be
added the need for investment capital and markets for
its exports before Western Europe can look forward to
the economic good health which is the foundation of
successful political, spiritual and defensive integration.
It is inevitable that the volume of East-West trade will
increase as American aid dries up and especially if we
will not, by a policy of trade reform, provide better and
more reliable access to the American market.

The important thing is that Europe's anxiety has had
the positive effect of helping to unify it. There are
heartening signs that the political stability and economic
vitality of Europe are to be fostered, not in separate
geographic units artificially created by conquest or mar-
riage, but as a whole. For the one situation in Europe

that can support an adequate living is Europe itself. An optimist might indeed prophesy that under the pressure of necessity the divisive spirit of nationalism that was born in Europe will die in Europe—with consequences that bode well for enduring resistance to the compulsory unification of communism.

But I strongly suspect that we in America are destined to endure in prolonged and irritable impatience the glacial pace of European integration. And we shall be perplexed and as always impatient with the manifestations of the new forces emerging in Europe: the persistence of large and bold Communist minorities in France and Italy; increasing trade with Russia, China and the satellites; and, of course, the assertiveness of growing self-confidence.

I think we have come to understand better the reasons for the parliamentary instability in peace-hungry France and Italy and the former's stubborn reluctance to face the reality of a threat greater than Germany. But persistence of large Communist political parties in these countries, to which they have become accustomed, makes it hard for them to understand our extreme anxiety about Communists, and in turn creates a complacency which exasperates us who are taxing and spending so heavily to help them fight communism. The explanation, in part at least, is that we don't have the same focus.

We are thinking of different things. When we think of "a Communist" we in America think of a hard core, malevolent conspirator dedicated to the overthrow of our government by intrigue if possible and force if necessary. Most Europeans, on the other hand, think of a neighbor, friend, fellow worker or even relative who votes Communist not to express his approval or preference for the Soviet system, but to express his disapproval of the conditions in which he lives and works.

The poverty of the Italian peasant is familiar. Only now with the land reform and development programs is the traditional Italian feudalism breaking up and the intolerable misery of millions abating. In France more than 80 per cent of the housing in the industrial slums was built before our Civil War. In Paris more than 100,000 young couples have no home of their own and little hope of one. The areas of overcrowding, tuberculosis, low income and misery are the areas of Communist strength among masses of people who have been waiting for reform, change and hope—not just for years but for generations. In Catholic Italy the pattern is similar. And to many observers the strange thing is that well-organized, well-financed and disciplined Communist party leadership has been able to do so little with this European legacy of economic stagnation, social irresponsibility, and the shocking disparity between rich and poor.

In our time, the American economy has been constantly changing, constantly converting higher productivity into higher wages, lower prices and greater consumption. We do not, to be sure, have a monopoly on such progress. The recovery of Western Germany since the war, and the way in which that divided and battered country has pressed on to new heights of income and output, is one of the remarkable economic achievements of our time. Britain, the Benelux and the Scandinavian countries have made steady progress and have shown that free people, by their own free decision, can arrange a wide and equitable distribution of the fruits of their common labors. However, elsewhere in Western Europe the picture is less bright. France has been suffering— as has Italy—from the tensions and the rigidities of a traditional capitalism. There one senses the ancient conflict of the "haves" and the "have nots." There social indifference and economies organized around low consumption mean that many people see little chance of bettering themselves and see little hope that their children will have a better life than their own.

However, for all the groans, excursions and lamentations, Europe is, I believe, groping along the path toward unity and strength. Where communism still exerts its influence, it is largely an influence bred in domestic distress which can be remedied, or an influence founded in the dismal conviction that Soviet power is the wave of the future and will inevitably win—and this can be remedied too.

In Western Europe, then, the power struggle appears to be in uneasy balance, with prospects for substantial improvement, and so far as the war of ideas is concerned, Moscow's influence and attraction are ebbing.

But in Asia the situation is reversed. For there the contest is primarily ideological and it would be a bold man indeed who would say that the peril is past and the outcome certain. For Asia is in revolution. Civilizations are very old, but political independence is very young. In the new states the economies are shaky, public administration is weak; they are hungry and poor, sensitive and proud. Nationalism is rampant. And the West, identified with the hated colonialism, is suspect. Utterly occupied with their own overwhelming problems, Asians see little of the world conflict with communism. But they know from experience a lot about colonialism, feudalism, landlords, moneylenders and oppressors, and the theories of Karl Marx sound pretty good to many of their leaders and intellectuals, who know surprisingly little about the ugly realities of communism in practice. Nor is there the perception one would expect of international communism as a new imperialism and a new threat to their independence.

There is little tradition of democracy in these new states, but independence, won at long last, is a passion, which partly accounts in some quarters for their opaque view of Communist China, where to many Asians it appears that the white invaders have at last been thrown out and the ignominy of centuries erased by Asians. There remains a reverent admiration for the ideas of the American Revolution, the Bill of Rights and the great utterances of national independence and human freedom. But they think they see in the current fears and excesses of anti-Communist zeal here at home a contradiction of our professions of faith in individual freedom. So also our alliance and friendship with the Western colonial powers seem to them to make our professed devotion to independence and self-determination hypocritical.

The contest of ideas doesn't mean much to the masses. And our anti-Communist preaching wins few hearts. The Asians want to know what we are for, not just what we are against. And in nations like India, Indonesia and Burma they don't accept the thesis that everyone must choose sides, that they have to be for us or against us, any more than we ourselves did in the midst of threats to world peace and freedom until a dozen or so years ago.

But in spite of all their doubts and difficulties the devotion of the leaders of Asia to the democratic idea of government by consent rather than force is impressive, as is the decisive manner in which so many of the new countries of Asia have dealt with violent Communist insurrections and conspiracies. Their revolutions have not produced Utopia, and they are struggling with infinite difficulties to raise living standards and satisfy the rising tide of expectations. They want rice and respect, and they want to believe in wondrous America that sends money and friendly, earnest people to help them, and that believes in them, and the aspirations of all God's children for peace, dignity and freedom.

Our people and our policy would be deeply concerned with these lands if Marx, Lenin and Stalin had never lived. For poverty, oppression and ignorance have always been our concern, and those who see virtue only in self-interest and self-preservation mistake, I think, our character and misread our history. Besides a policy and attitude narrowly based on self-interest alone will lift no hearts and win no minds in Asia.

A propitious political accident, however, has made our inborn compassion co-ordinate with the national interest; and happily so, for in an area that has known so much of colonialism and condescension, compassion and humility will be our greatest asset in the struggle for the minds of men and the allegiance of uncommitted nations in the decisive area of Asia.

Lenin said "the road to Paris lies through Peiping and Delhi," and the Moscow-Peiping axis will not yield the road to Western ideas and allegiance without an epic struggle for Asia that will sorely try our forbearance, understanding and magnanimity. We shall have to avoid the sins of self-righteousness and self-delusion. Our power is not absolute, nor is our judgment infallible. If we act as if we had a monopoly on all strength and all truth, we will soon discover that ours is the monopoly of hopeless isolation. The tempered use of our power, the sympathetic understanding of people's "yearning to breathe free," the modest proffer of our ideas and faith— these constitute the true resources of America and the treasured hope of our civilization.

Until the long labor is achieved, perpetual peril will be our lot and our condition.

America's Burden

I HAVE suggested that the emergence in Russia of predatory communism does not wholly explain the ferment of change that has convulsed, distorted and re-shaped our twentieth-century world. And the elimination of communism as an aggressive, expansive world movement would by no means restore tranquillity, order and security. There would still be with us both the old problem of Russian expansion as well as the new problem of the awakening of continents.

A hundred and fifty years ago Russian leaders were saying that "the mass of Turkish territories in Europe should be divided into separate states, governed locally and bound to each other by a federation, upon which Russia would be able to secure herself a decisive and lawful influence by means of the title of Emperor or Protector of the Slavs of the East which would be accorded to his Imperial Majesty."

What was foreseen 150 years ago has come to pass. Much of that "mass of Turkish territories in Europe," and far more besides, has fallen under Russian control and "satellite" is our Western synonym for what those earlier Russian leaders called "decisive influence." Russian expansion into the Far East, which began even earlier, still goes on, but under slogans and labels better adapted to the modern social revolution. I suspect the Czars would see little new, surprising or distasteful in the aggressions of their successors in the Kremlin. Indeed, reflecting on the frustration of their own plans by the containment policies of nineteenth-century Europe, they might even feel obliged to congratulate the Communist usurpers for their spectacular successes.

It is interesting and perhaps instructive to recall that the Bolshevik Revolution of 1917 was avowedly anti-imperialist; that it renounced the traditional imperial Russian expansionism. But it was not long before the anti-imperialism of the founders of political communism was in turn abandoned and the new Soviet Union reverted to the ancient policies of Imperial Russia.

Two factors perhaps have contributed to our imperfect perception of this continuity in Russian history. For years after the revolution the leaders in the Kremlin were busy perfecting their system, consolidating their position at home, building up the economic and military power of a backward country, catching up with the technological advances of the West, and organizing the world Communist movement. Then we were diverted for some years by the devastating bursts of expansion by violence in Germany, Italy and Japan.

But now, after pausing for revolution, modernization and world war, a stronger Russia is at it again, and we are compelled once more to face the old and half-forgotten reality of Russia's implacable expansionism. Moreover, it seems both reasonable and prudent to assume that the leaders of Russia, whoever they are, will persist in this policy by force or guile until the new age of political enlightenment dawns in the Kremlin.

(One wonders, indeed, if there is a counterpart in the Far East, if Korea and Indo-China are evidence of a re-awakened imperial spirit in the new Communist China; one wonders if they imply an approach to problems beyond China's borders which adds revolution to the old Chinese imperial concept of what they called the "tribute states" of Vietnam, Siam, Burma, Korea and parts of Malaya and Indonesia. It seems not unlikely that all of these states and Laos and Cambodia are on Red China's satellite list to insure the security of the borders and the economic well being of the vast homeland.)

At all events, while Russian behavior is consistent with its history, it is clear that something new has been added, and that the new faith of communism is a potent weapon for conquest of the peasant and industrial proletariat, the oppressed and the miserable, especially where poverty is the rule and the recollections of colonialism are painful and fresh. While the promises of emancipation and liberation and the ultimate triumph of socialism and the Communist "people's paradise" are for export only, as the sufferers in all the Russian-occupied countries know so well, the appeal is great to the ignorant and aggrieved. A failure to recognize and to combat the momentum of Russian and Chinese expansion, arrayed in communism's seductive panoply of deliverance for the masses of the Middle East, Asia and Africa, could lose to Western civilization vast areas and peoples which are not dispensable.

As I have pointed out, this fateful struggle in the East is essentially ideological and the burden falls largely on the United States. In the nineteenth century Europe concerted its power to contain Russia. Now this can no longer be done even in Europe, let alone in Asia. As it has fallen to our lot to redress the balance of power in Europe, the hope of security for ourselves, let alone the salvation of the millions who yearn for freedom, devolves on us even more in the East where the Western empires and sources of power have gone with the winds of war and rebellion, and left behind bitter memories of the white man's colonialism and paternalism.

While any inventory of the West's assets and liabilities in the Asian conflict is beyond the scope of this discussion and of my competence, its complexity in comparison with Europe is apparent to any traveler. In Europe the tradition of national independence is old and the more recent development of political democracy rests on a broad basis of literacy, political consciousness and relatively high standards of living. But in the East independence is new, the economies weak, illiteracy high, societies agrarian and stratified, poverty universal, and political consciousness confined to a thin layer. In such circumstances the evolution of the revolution in an orderly way toward the goals of tolerable living standards and the Western democratic concept of government by consent would be difficult and slow at best. But it is made much more difficult and hazardous by Communist interference, incitement, falsehood and pressure.

If anticolonialism and independence are the root passions of the Asian revolution one wonders, sometimes in despair, why international communism should be any problem at all, why with all of Eastern Europe as mute witnesses Asians don't perceive at once that their real enemy is the new Communist imperialism and not the vanishing empires of the West. We can point to the revival of Russia's historical expansionism; we can point to China's seizure of Tibet, invasion of Korea, invasion by proxy of Indo-China, Communist insurrections in Malaya, the Philippines, Burma, Indonesia, and to the built-in fifth columns among the 13 million Chinese living throughout Southeast Asia. We can point, finally, to the consequences of Communist conquest—slavery for the people, submission to the central authority of Moscow or Peiping, and the quick extinction of the dream of genuine national independence. If they point to Yugoslavia's independence of Moscow we can ask them to speculate where Yugoslavia would be were it not for Western help. And we can remind them that China is a next-door neighbor to all of East Asia.

But we have not yet wholly succeeded in clearly identifying the real threat; we have not yet succeeded in marshaling the massive forces of independence against the real enemy. Why not? Can it be done? Can it be done in time? How? These are questions which will plague us for years to come. And if the central problems of the power struggle in Western Europe—the future of Germany, an expanding economy, social reconstruction and unification—are perplexing, they seem relatively simple compared to Asia where we cannot expect to make much progress in the building of a more stable power relationship while the ideological struggle is still going on among many states, races and religions.

There are many reasons why perception of the real danger of Communist imperialism is not as distinct in the East as in the West and why, therefore, the ideological struggle is more apparent in Asia than in Europe and its outcome less predictable. Because they are so numerous I will mention only a few of them to indicate the dimensions of the difficulties facing the free world's defenders.

In the first place, of course, is colonialism. It is hard, especially for Americans, to appreciate the depth of this feeling. For centuries resentments have been accumulating among sensitive, proud and ancient peoples for the indignities, exploitation and injuries, real or fancied, of the white man's rule. It will be a long time before this feeling is erased, but it can be reduced. The present cordial relations between Indians and Pakistanis and their former masters, the British, were to me one of the marvels of the East, and evidence of what can be done.

Some of the deep-seated hostility to Western pretensions and condescension has rubbed off on us in spite of our liberation of the Philippines and our traditional anti-imperialism. But curiously it does not seem to rub off on the Russians, probably in part because they are exceedingly inconspicuous in comparison with the Americans who are numerous, visible and closely allied and identified with the Western European colonialists. Also it should be remembered that Russia is not a newcomer to Asia; it wasn't brought into Asia by President Roosevelt at Yalta, as some of us seem to think. It has been a great Asian power for 200 years and includes many Asian peoples. It was a part of Asia long before the advent of communism, and the Asian evidently doesn't think of Russians when he think and talks of European colonialism.

Moreover, the Russians understand the Orientals, their languages and how they think, better than we, who have a tendency everywhere to expect others to think and act as we do and to appreciate our disinterested and philanthropic righteousness. Finally, it is hard for many peoples, far removed from the struggle in the West, to see any military threat to their independence from a Russia lying beyond the borders of distant Manchuria and the high Himalayas.

The Soviet Union may be far away but political communism is not; and there are no leaders in the new lands anywhere who have not had incessant troubles with native Communist political movements. As I have said, the appeal of Marxist thought is considerable in Asia and even among the leaders, Western-oriented by education and democratic by conviction, there are wonder and respect for the Soviet achievement in industrialization and the rapid development of their country. For the basic problem of most of the newly independent under-developed areas is how to match with performance the promises of their revolutions; how to increase literacy and public health; how to develop their natural resources and reclaim waste areas; how to improve the production of agricultural commodities and consumer goods; how in short, to bring off a delayed industrial revolution and improve the people's lot, quickly—and with little domestic capital and limited national resources to do it.

It is a formidable task to say the least, and it is hardly surprising that the Soviet Union's spectacular achievement in similar circumstances attracts admiring attention and curiosity. Whether the job can be done by the Western methods of consent, or whether impatience, agitation and discontent will drive them to the methods of force and brutal dictatorship, is the big issue. And it is precisely here in the field of economic development and internal improvement where the West and the United States have the advantage both in means and technical experience.

Stability and indigenous strength in what remains of free Asia can only be established in the long run by the will and work of the people themselves. Neither American nor United Nations money, technicians nor advice in any amount is likely to be decisive. But we can help others not just to understand better the deadly deceptions of imperial communism but also to deal more effectively with their own problems and to help themselves. We can contribute greatly to economic improvement and political stability, and to the evolution of healthy governments capable of defending their own interests against outside domination. Indeed we have already done so. But to limit our effort to military strength alone, or to make economic aid contingent on military co-operation, or to penalize and abuse the neutralist nations would be to ignore the basic fact that in large areas of the Middle East, Asia and Africa we have not yet resolved the ideological conflict. Before a reliable and effective defense community can be created there has to be a community purpose.

In Asia, now, India and Japan are the anchors of the free world. With them rests the balance of power; as they are strong and free their non-Communist neighbors will draw increased strength and confidence in the alternative to China and communism. Hence they are the obvious Communist objectives. If either falls most of Asia will be vulnerable and the Communist conspirators will be in sight of their goal of a soft and sympathetic Asia, a neutralized Europe and an isolated America.

India, both because of its decisive weight in South and

Southeast Asia and because it is ideologically and militarily less defensible than Japan, appears to be first on
the flexible Communist schedule. The noisy partisan
search for scapegoats that has demeaned the American
political scene since the Communist conquest of China
will be but a preview of the dismal drama—"Who Lost
India?"—if enormous India with its enormous problems
slips under the Iron Curtain. Responsible and popular
opinion in India is deeply anti-Communist as of now. But
they don't want us to save them from communism, and
there is still some ambivalence about acceptance of help
which they think has more to do with power politics than
with genuine good will and generosity. They want and
need and know they need help, but they are also sensitive
and sad that it must be so; that they have gained independence and are still dependent.

In addition to the democratic convictions of the new
India's leaders there are many other factors working
against communism: the tolerance of the Hindu for other
ideas, the individualism of the villagers, Gandhi's philosophy of nonviolence, the heritage of British justice, order
and responsible government, the large five-year plan for
development and economic improvement, and so forth.

But there are many negative factors too, and India's
unrealistic but persistent neutralism has been particularly
irritating to us. I doubt if the tolerant attitude toward

China is so much a reflection of moral indecision or ideological sympathy for communism as an expression of Asian and anticolonial solidarity. But Indians, whether sentimentally bemused or trying to avoid taking sides for practical reasons, must be rapidly learning the facts about life with world communism. And the more they see of situations like the prisoner-of-war conflict in Korea, Communist activity in their own country and along their northern borders, and the more closely Mao follows the Stalinist lead, the more rapidly India's education in realities will spread and her illusions vanish.

We must face the fact that throughout the East the central problem is the attraction and growing power of Communist China. For the first time since British and other naval vessels forced open China's ports to Western trade a century ago, the mainland Chinese, some 500 millions, are now organized under vigorous, fanatical leadership. The Japanese and the Germans have demonstrated the power potential of much smaller and geographically less secure nations when effectively mobilized and industrialized. And that is what China is now doing with Russian and East European help. The spectacular development in thirty-five years of the Soviet Union, today the world's second industrial power, is a sobering reminder of what ruthless totalitarianism can do. China may in time become an even greater influence for good or evil in the

world than its partner in the vast Chinese-Russian heartland stretching from the Danube to the Pacific. And
someone may yet write a piece or give a lecture entitled
"Will Malenkov Become A Tito?"

As young men many of the leaders in Peiping felt the
humiliation of the "treaty era" when Westerners treated
Chinese as inferiors. The leaders of Communist China
now appear to be motivated by multiple compulsions to
(1) liberate fellow Asians from what they call "imperialist
domination and feudalism," (2) and, as they say, "right
the wrongs done China by the Western powers" and
restore the nation to her "rightful" status in Asia and
the world, and (3) forestall Western-supported action
against the Communist regime by creating situations
that make such action less possible.

In Asia the intangible weight of probable Communist
mistakes is on our side. The Chinese may prove much
wiser and cleverer than the Russians under Stalin, but if
they perform in the manner of their senior Soviet partners
it is predictable that their pressure and obstinacy will alert
and arouse the free Asians, even as Soviet intransigence
awakened and united Western Europe. Indeed, it is likely
that the wholesale defection of Chinese prisoners-of-war
in Korea followed by the enlarged operations in Indo-
China is spreading the alarm.

The assumption is reasonable and all the evidence

confirms that the leaders of Communist China intend to follow the Soviet example and press forward toward their goal of an industrialized and militarily powerful state. But however ruthless and bloodthirsty Mao and his lieutenants may be, to maintain party unity and organize on the centralized Communist system a vast, sprawling, overpopulated empire with primitive communications and limited natural resources is a monstrous undertaking.

While in the past Asian policy of Imperial Russia and even of the Soviets has been little influenced by a feeble, divided China on the other side of the longest boundary in the world, henceforth it is obvious that relations with her Communist neighbor will be a major Soviet concern. One could point out many interesting possibilities here, but I will not speculate on future Soviet-Chinese relations. The only safe assumption for the present, at least, is that they will continue firm and cordial. And there is little doubt that the Soviet Union has made substantial contributions in goods and technical services to China's development, although there is no way of knowing what concessions have been exacted in return. But China's rapid industrial development would seem to require the greatest possible trade with the outside world and for years to come. It would also seem to require a long period of peace.

Our friends both in the East and West who are yearning for more trade point to China's ominous growing commercial dependence on Russia. The 80 million Japanese on their little islands must expand their commerce as our economic support declines. The Germans and British, too, seem to be more eager if anything than Peiping to reopen the trade channels with China. If we don't choose to make markets available here and if we terminate economic aid to our allies, the China market will become more attractive to the nations who must trade to live, and who are also important members of the defensive coalition against communism.

China has it in her power to decide whether and how long the French will bleed in Indo-China and whether and how long we must hold the lines in Korea. To the gathering problems of Indo-China, Korea, Formosa and admission to the United Nations, we shall have to add the rising pressure from our friends for more trade. Hastening industrial development will enhance the strength of China in the Orient, but there is danger too in opposing what our allies need without offering them—as in the trade question—an economic alternative.

All of which highlights the difficulties of leadership, and the further danger of a weakened coalition with the assumption of unilateral responsibilities by a progressively isolated United States. Unilateralism in turn will encourage false hopes at home and neutralism abroad;

it will tend to confirm the Communist charge that our purpose is not disinterested co-operation but self-interested domination. The United States will soon have to formulate a reasoned policy with respect to China. We will shortly have to evolve the minimum conditions on which we are willing to live and let live with the Chinese Communists, with the probability that, as in Europe, the ideological contest will go on for a long time.

I have tried to point out that much of the world in Asia, Africa and the Middle East is on the way—somewhere; is trying to telescope centuries into decades, trying to catch up with the Western industrial and technological revolutions overnight and under much more difficult circumstances. And they are trying to accomplish this mighty transformation by the methods of consent, not coercion. A policy based just on anti-communism and military potency is not in the spirit of this great movement of the twentieth century and will win few hearts. The challenge for us is to identify ourselves with this social and human revolution, to encourage, aid and inspire the aspirations of half of mankind for a better life, to guide these aspirations into paths that lead to freedom. To default would be disaster.

The great issue that splits the world in this troubled age, the issue of tyranny or freedom, cannot be reconciled. But need it be forced to a decision? It seems to me the problem is not to find ways to live in harmony with the adversary; it is to find ways to live beside him in the bitter discord of incessant power and ideological competition. In time there will be a break, sooner perhaps than prudence admits.

The infinity of problems we now face, and I have tried to suggest but some of them and their genesis, cannot all be solved quickly. And some of our problems probably can't be solved at all. Our choice is to let time assuage or exacerbate. Emotion in matters of national security is no substitute for intelligence, nor rigidity for prudence. To act coolly, intelligently and prudently in perilous circumstances is the test of a man or nation. The responsibility for organizing and sustaining the great coalition befell us Americans suddenly and before we were prepared for it. But we shall have to learn this job quickly and well. As foreign policy grows out of historical experience and reflects national character, perhaps it is not irrelevant to this task to consider some aspects of our national character and experience.

One of our hardest tasks—if we hope to conduct a successful foreign policy—is to learn a new habit of thought, a new attitude toward the problems of life itself. Fortitude, sobriety and patience as a prescription for combating intolerable evil are cold porridge to Americans who yesterday tamed a continent and tipped the scales decisively in two world wars. Americans have always assumed, subconsciously, that all problems can be solved; that every story has a happy ending; that the application of enough energy and good will can make everything come out right. In view of our history, this assumption is natural enough. As a people, we have never encountered any obstacle that we could not overcome. The Pilgrims had a rough first winter, but after that the colony flourished. Valley Forge was followed naturally by Yorktown. Daniel Boone always found his way through the forest. We crossed the Alleghenies and the Mississippi and the Rockies with an impetus that nothing could stop. The wagon trains got through; the Pony Express delivered the mail; in spite of Bull Run and the Copperheads, the Union was somehow preserved. We never came across a river we couldn't bridge, a depression we couldn't overcome, a war we couldn't win. So far, we have never known the tragedy, frustration and sometimes defeat which are ingrained in the memories of all other peoples.

So when we encounter a problem in foreign policy we naturally assume that it can be solved pretty quick, with enough drive, determination and red corpuscles. "The difficult we do immediately, the impossible takes a little longer." Just pour in enough man power, money and bulldozers, and we can lick it. If one diplomat can't come up with the answer, fire him and hire another—or better yet, hire ten. And if that doesn't solve it, some Americans conclude that there can be only one explanation: treason.

And this raises the question of foreign policy by hindsight. Obviously the British withdrawal from India in 1947 created a power vacuum in that area which was very pleasing to the Kremlin. But did the Conservatives for political advantage charge the Labour government with selling Britain down the river, or being dupes or fellow travelers? Of course not. Remembering the follies of the Chamberlain regime, did Churchill exclude men of Munich from the wartime Cabinet? Of course not. But in our country in recent years we have repeatedly seen policies developed without protest at one time which turned out unsuccessfully, in whole or in part, attacked at a later time for partisan advantage as bumbling and fumbling and even betrayal or treachery. And thereby the door is opened not only to political foul play and demagoguery but to the destruction of public confidence at home and moral authority abroad. No administration can conduct a sound foreign policy when the future sits in judgment on the past and officials are held accountable as dupes, fools or traitors for anything that goes wrong.

Such extreme and cynical political irresponsibility is a problem for the electorate and the press, I suppose,

which means that it is a problem of education and character for us. And so are impatience, arrogance and our
faith in quick solutions.

As long as this habit of mind persists—and it is funda-
mentally an unchristian attitude, ignoring the pervasive-
ness of evil and loaded with arrogance and pride—we
shall never be able to face our problems realistically.
Our first job, it seems to me, is to school ourselves in
cold-eyed humility; to recognize that our wisdom is imperfect and that our capabilities are limited.

Many of the really hard problems in international relations may never be "solved" at all. The conflict between
Moslem and Christian, which dominated world politics
for some 300 years, was never resolved. Islam and Chris-
tianity learned to live together and the problem was
submerged in the newer and more urgent problems of
the Renaissance, the Age of Discovery, and finally the
Industrial Revolution. So with the Thirty Years' War,
which also started as a conflict between two ideologies,
Protestant and Catholic. The underlying issues were
never settled because they were logically irreconcilable;
but they did cease to preoccupy the minds of men, as
nationalism and class conflict began to emerge as more
pressing issues. Before that war finally petered out,
curiously enough, a Catholic Cardinal—Richelieu—was
organizing the Protestant League, and a Protestant gen-

eral was leading the armies of the Holy Roman Empire. The struggle had been transformed from one of religious ideology to one of national ambition.

It is at least conceivable that the ideological conflicts of our own time will defy solution, in similar fashion, but will be replaced by other problems which we cannot now foresee.

So the first step in learning our new role in world affairs is not one which can be taken by technicians in the State Department, or even by political leaders. It has to be taken by individual Americans, in the privacy of their own homes, hearts and souls. It involves a conscious acceptance of Christian humility—a recognition that we are never going to solve many of the hard problems of the world, but will simply have to learn to live with them, for years and maybe for centuries.

When we have accomplished that step, we will no longer call out a posse to find the traitor who was responsible for "our" loss of China; or threaten the French with dire punishment if they don't stop behaving like Frenchmen forthwith. We will no longer be tempted by simple panaceas and total solutions—a blockade of China, or an arms burden that may crush necessary social changes in weak economies and deliver them to the enemy, or unlimited billions for Point Four, or whatever.

On the latter point don't misunderstand me. Point

Four and technical assistance are good medicine, in doses which can be absorbed by responsible and genuinely representative governments. However, I am not one of those who think that economic aid is a miracle drug and a sure cure for all ailments, and especially when it is allocated and judged here at home not on its value in building stable, democratic societies, but on its effectiveness in winning a country, India for example, to our side. As I have indicated, I think conformity with our views and defensive alliances, while highly desirable, is generally not the cause but the consequence of government that has the support of the people so that they will want to defend it against external aggression or internal subversion. It is hard and futile to defend a government whose people won't defend it. We shall have to learn that we cannot buy agreement or effective alliances among the new states of the Middle East and Asia with economic or military aid. All we can do, and in my judgment must do, is to help with the building of free and independent governments whose people will defend them.

All of us, as individuals, have to learn much the same lessons as we approach maturity. In youth, everything seems possible; but we reach a point in the middle years when we realize that we are never going to reach all the shining goals we had set for ourselves. And in the end, most of us reconcile ourselves, with what grace we can, to living with our ulcers and arthritis, our sense of partial failure, our less-than-ideal families—and even our politicians! Maybe America, as a nation, is approaching that point. Maybe we are just now going through that period of emotional protest—so common with individuals in early middle age—which precedes the acceptance of the sad realities of mature responsibility.

In passing, it is noteworthy that other nations have greater patience, especially the Communist ones; and this puts us with our obsessive need for quick solutions at a disadvantage. The Chinese, Russians, Persians, and even British don't mind negotiating for weeks or even years, if necessary. But maybe we too are learning; certainly we showed a good deal of patience in the Korean armistice negotiations, for example. In this connection, however, there would seem to be manifest impatience and even disregard of our friends in such recent impulsive and ill-starred diplomatic maneuvers as the Trieste "solution," the "new look," "massive retaliation," and the sudden cry for "united action" in Indo-China, where a war has been going on and going badly for seven years.

The ordeal of our times, I have suggested, is a challenge to American maturity and American responsibility. Nowhere is this testing more fundamental than in the field of the free mind. For never has an external threat required more clear-headed analysis, more hard and sober thought and more bold and unterrified vision than the threat we confront today. And yet the very existence of that threat has created strains and tensions, anguish and anxiety, which beat upon the free mind, surround it, torment it, and threaten to smother it. It is an irony that unreason should never be more manifest than in the midst of our great planetary effort to make freedom secure.

Senator Fulbright has called anti-intellectualism "that swinish blight so common in our time." This infection has been epidemic, of course, in the totalitarian states. Antireason is the spirit of the shouting, chanting crowds we remember so well in Hitler's Germany. Almost daily we read of new manifestations of unreason, mob emotion and violence in some part of the world. In recent years we have even seen the contagion of unreason and anti-intellectualism spreading among ourselves, inhibiting thought and initiative in government, distorting the emphasis in our public affairs, moving groups to extremes of intolerance, diverting attention from our great concerns and provoking division among us.

Unreason and anti-intellectualism abominate thought. Thinking implies disagreement; and disagreement implies nonconformity; and nonconformity implies heresy; and heresy implies disloyalty—so, obviously, thinking must be stopped. But shouting is not a substitute for thinking and reason is not the subversion but the salvation of freedom.

Another lesson that we shall have to learn is that we cannot deal with questions of foreign policy in terms of moral absolutes. Compromise is not immoral or treasonable. It is the objective of negotiation and negotiation is the means of resolving conflict peacefully. But when we negotiate we have to have something to negotiate *with* as well as *for*. If rigidity and absolutist attitudes deprive our representatives of anything to negotiate *with* then there is nothing they can negotiate *for*. The consequences can be very embarrassing.

We seem to have a current illustration of self-defeating rigidity in the case of China. Because of our justified moral revulsion to the bloodthirsty conspiracy in China, the competition in extreme opinions and arbitrary attitudes among political leaders has virtually deprived us of all flexibility. The Secretary of State was even severely criticized by his own party leaders for even agreeing to join our allies in a meeting with the Chinese. And rigidity known publicly in advance not only embarrasses us with our allies but can be seized upon by our enemies and advertised among the uncommitted peoples to prove our obdurate refusal to make any concessions for peace.

The point is not necessarily that we should support the

admission to the United Nations of China or grant recognition or something else in exchange for a settlement in Indo-China, Korea or Formosa. The point is that we must not be imprisoned by our own passions, propaganda or pronouncements; we should not tie the hands of our representatives and hobble ourselves in advance to the adversary's advantage, not ours.

Times change, and rapidly, in this era of change. John Stuart Mill wrote: "That which seems the height of absurdity in one generation often becomes the height of wisdom in the next." Not very long ago there was a lot of "radical" agitation, so called, in this country. What did the "radicals" want? They wanted social security, old age pensions, regulation of utilities and securities, government aid for housing and education, a nine-hour day and collective bargaining. Those were heresies not long ago but in 1953 a Republican President raises the welfare state to Cabinet status and asks for an extension of social security.

Similarly a few years ago we were fighting the Germans and Japanese tooth and toenail and calling them names not fit to print. Today we are nourishing them with our money and arming them with our weapons. A few years ago I was doing savage battle with the Communist Yugoslavs in the United Nations. But last summer the same people entertained me like a long lost friend from one end of Yugoslavia to the other.

Passions rise and subside. Absolutes are few and black and white rare colors in international politics. Keeping an open, flexible mind, shedding our passion for crusades and our taste for absolutes that equate compromise with immorality, will be another hard and useful exercise. As Churchill has said: "Guidance in these mundane matters is granted to us only step by step. . . . There is therefore wisdom in reserving one's decisions as long as possible and until all the facts and forces that will be potent are revealed."

The price of inflexibility in foreign policy will be loss of confidence in our leadership first, then the loss of our allies, or worse. We can't have things all our own way. We shall have to face the necessity of compromise not only with our allies but with our enemies, for power factors are realities. And we shall have to learn to expect something less than total success every time, and not slander our officials as suspicious characters at every setback or failure. For if we do we shall soon have no successes.

There are limits to the effectiveness of our nation's foreign policy. For foreign policy is concerned with problems which lie beyond our jurisdiction and about which we cannot legislate. There are only two means available for influencing the actions of other states: persuasion and coercion. As a free society, we must rely primarily on persuasion. We can use coercion only rarely, and usually only as a defensive measure. We cannot have satellites because this depends on the use of coercion. We cannot employ threats and intimidation effectively because our actions are open to free discussion and criticism. Great as our power is, we have only a marginal influence on developments outside our boundaries. Guatemala is an example. Our power is almost infinite in comparison to Guatemala's. Yet we have been unable to prevent the emergence of Communist influence there.

Like every great power we are always and simultaneously on both the defensive and the offensive. We must adjust our defense to the adversary's strength and should develop our offense to make the most of our strength. The defensive task is to work with our allies and friends to deny the adversary opportunities to win cheap successes. Communism has yet to gain power in any state through free elections. It must gain control of key positions of power by subversion, penetration, or violence—civil war as in Indo-China or direct aggression as in Korea. The defensive task is in large part a military task: to develop and maintain such strength as to deter general war and to deal with violence in local situations. It is partly a political and economic task; for example, military measures alone are inadequate in Indo-China and political and economic measures are necessary now to bring stability to Korea.

The offensive task is to work with allied and friendly countries to create a world environment favorable to the steady growth of free institutions. This means political arrangements which will make possible the unity of action essential to survival but which at the same time are consistent with diversity. It means a healthy international economy. The offensive task never ends. Progress will be slow. We hope that we can leave the world in a little better shape than we found it. But to search for a "solution" prematurely is more likely to produce war than peace. There is no such "solution" now, but our problems may fade away with time and cease to have the importance that they now seem to have.

Because of the nature of free societies, it is of the utmost importance to prevent war, if possible, and if this is not possible, to keep any future war as severely limited in scope as possible. It is a sign of strength, not of weakness, to be able to keep war limited. To generalize hostilities to a world scale would imperil the very institutions we seek to save by war.

Our objective is not the destruction of communism by war. Our objective is not the incitement of others to violence. Our objective is not to rectify the boundaries and correct the unnatural divisions that afflict the world by force, but by peaceful processes. Our objective is a peace consistent with decency and justice. And our prayer is that history will not say that we led a noble but a lost cause.

It is doubtful whether in all history two ways of life as different and opposed as the Communist way and our way of life have ever come into contact with one another at so many different points without engaging in mortal conflict.

Experience suggests that it has not been easy for men to learn the wisdom and virtue of tolerance for ideas and ways of life which deeply offend the cherished tenets of their own faith. In times past men of fervent faith regarded religious tolerance as a sign of moral weakness rather than moral strength. It seems that only when warring faiths have become convinced that they must choose between common survival and mutual extinction do they agree to live and let live.

Probably the greatest obstacle in the path of peaceful coexistence is the Soviet belief in the inevitability of conflict between the Communist and the non-Communist worlds. And it is true that Soviet intolerance and unwillingness to abide by the rules of peaceful coexistence have shaken our faith in tolerance and the possibility of peaceful coexistence. But in the atomic era even the most fanatical faith is likely to balk at self-destruction. There is no Iron Curtain that the aggregate sentiments of mankind cannot and will not penetrate in time. Even the most fanatical ambition must adjust itself to demonstrated truth or perish. No faith can long rest on the belief that the world is flat—if its adherents know the world is round. "Great is the truth and mighty above all things."

The hope for peaceful coexistence lies in our ability to convince the rulers of the other world that they cannot extend their system by force, or by stealth, and that unless they use force against us we will not use force against them; that our coalition exists but to serve and to save the imperishable principles of the Charter of the United Nations.

Intolerant power respects power, not weakness. It is imperative therefore to build and better the balance of power. Conspiracy and incitement prosper in disunion and discontent. It is imperative therefore to build and better the unity and well being of the free world. We cannot do it alone. It is imperative therefore to build and better the coalition. And here we encounter our greatest danger and our final task. A coalition built on expedient reaction to the common danger will not stand, because the Sino-Soviet alliance has the power to blow hot and cold, like Boreas and Phoebus in the fable; it has the power to relax or increase the tension as it sees fit. But our coalition cannot live by fits and starts; it must rest on an enduring community of interest. And successful communal relations mean give and take, co-operation, consultation, accommodation—a decent respect for the opinions of others. Our coalition is a partnership, not a dictatorship. We shall have to listen as well as talk; learn as well as teach. And I sometimes think that what America needs more than anything else is a hearing aid. We can encourage the acceptance of our ideas only as we are willing to accept the ideas and suggestions of others. All of this means a large relinquishment of our freedom of action.

There is not the slightest chance of confidence and mutual trust among the members of the free world's coalition if the United States should fail the test of leadership. We have a great and fortuitous advantage, for if there is nothing the Kremlin wants more than to rule the world, there is nothing the United States wants less than to rule the world. To cling to that truth with clarity, sincerity and humility will be our greatest strength in the trials of leadership.

America's greatest contribution to human society has come not from her wealth or weapons or ambitions, but from her ideas; from the moral sentiments of human liberty and human welfare embodied in the Declaration of Independence and the Bill of Rights. We must cling to these truths, for these are everlasting and universal aspirations. In the words of Lincoln: "It was not the mere separation of the colonies from the motherland, but the sentiment in the Declaration of Independence which gave liberty not alone to the people of this country, but hope to all the world. It was that which gave promise that in due time the weights should be lifted from the shoulders of all men, and that all should have an equal chance." Throughout its history, America has given hope, comfort and inspiration to freedom's cause in all lands. The reservoir of good will and respect for America was not built up by American arms or intrigue; it was built upon our deep dedication to the cause of human liberty and human welfare.

All through human history runs a struggle between right and wrong, which is destined to endure, perhaps, to the end of time. Some historians during our materialistic years disavowed this theme. But now in our age of anxiety and time of testing, they are bringing it again within their purview. Arthur Schlesinger, Jr., has stated: "If historians are to understand the fullness of the social dilemma they seek to reconstruct, they must understand that sometimes there is no escape from the implacabilities of moral decisions"; while Allan Nevins notes with approval the emergence in historical writing of "a deepened moral sense much needed in our troubled age."

If the record of man's progress is the chronicle of everlasting struggle between right and wrong, it follows that the solutions of our problems lie largely within ourselves, that only with self-mastery can we hope to master history. The scientific mastery of our environment has brought us not tranquillity but rather unrest and new fears. Knowledge alone is not enough. It must be leavened with magnanimity before it becomes wisdom. And "magnanimity in politics," as Burke has reminded us, "is not seldom the truest wisdom."

America's life story is the record of a marvelous growth of body, mind and character. Now at maturity we shoulder the heaviest burdens of greatness, for in the last analysis the epic struggle for our civilization, for government by consent of the governed, will be determined by what Americans are capable of. In bearing burdens, in ennobling new duties of citizenship, is the greatness of men and nations measured, not in pomp and circumstance.

How shall we bear what Providence has assigned us? In Keat's *Hyperion* are these lines:

> for to bear all naked truths,
> And to envisage circumstances, all calm,
> That is the top of sovereignty. . . .

And so it is.

EDWIN LAWRENCE GODKIN
1831–1902

Edwin Lawrence Godkin, editor of *The Nation* and the New
York *Evening Post*, was born in Ireland of English stock, and
took his degree at Queen's College, Belfast, in 1951. He published a *History of Hungary* and was associated with the London
Daily News and the Belfast *Northern Whig* before coming to
America in 1856. Here his letters to the *Daily News* on American
public affairs attracted attention and prepared him for the task
he assumed in 1865 as first editor of *The Nation*, to which he
gave a scholarly quality, a breadth of view, and a moral tone that
brought it recognition as one of the best weeklies in the English-
speaking world. In 1881 *The Nation* became the weekly edition
of the New York *Evening Post* of which Godkin was made
editor in chief in 1883. From that time until his retirement in
1900 he exercised an influence on public opinion out of all
proportion to the circulation of his paper. Editors throughout the
country, whether in sympathy with his views or not, watched
for his editorials on all important issues. He was exceptionally
well read in economics, history and political theory, believed
whole-heartedly in democracy, owed allegiance to no person or
party, and was vigorous and fearless in expression. In 1903, by a
gift to Harvard University, his friends established "The Godkin
Lectures on the Essentials of Free Government and the Duties
of the Citizen" in appreciation of his long and disinterested
service to the country of his adoption and in the hope of stimulat-
ing that spirit of independent thought and devotion to the public
service which characterized his career.

Set in Linotype Electra
Format by D. F. Bradley
Manufactured by The Haddon Craftsmen, Inc.
Published by HARPER & BROTHERS, New York